HIGHER FREQUENCIES

HIGHER FREQUENCIES

JOURNEY TO ENLIGHTENMENT

Isaiah Sky Orlen

Higher Frequencies Global LLC

Contents

Discipline your senses to purify your mind, body, and soul through your spiritual practice, nutritional behavior, physical fitness routine, and relationship with self and others.

Journey toward enlightenment by immersing in higher frequencies and transformative modalities that awaken the human connection to divine consciousness.

I am not a doctor, I am not a guru, I am not a shaman, I am not a scientist; I am someone who has walked through the fire of life only to realize that I am the fire. Through this dance I have educated and healed myself with a unique blend of spirituality, physical fitness, and nutritional behavior, allowing me to heal my relationship with myself and others. I have created my own school of thought from books, podcasts, lectures, higher education, and various faiths. And through this process I have found a weaving of healing that I feel is my mission to share with all those I encounter who are receptive. It is irrelevant to me if this helps one or one million people, so long as it helps anyone's heart it touches on their journey to enlightenment.

I am not the message but merely the messenger.

I am a warrior, I am a magician, I am a healer.

I am divine consciousness…

And so are you

My hope is that my journey and the following pages serves as a guide to rediscover, enhance, and connect you to the light within you….

Stay Blessed, Stay Grateful, Stay Appreciative,

And Love without the want of reciprocity.

About the Book

What if enlightenment wasn't a destination—but a frequency you could tune into?

In *Higher Frequencies: Journey to Enlightenment*, author and visionary Isaiah Sky Orlen guides readers on a transformative path of self-mastery—drawing from timeless spiritual wisdom, modern consciousness studies, and regenerative healing practices.

Through the lens of the Victim, Survivor, and Warrior archetypes, Orlen breaks down the *Higher Frequencies* mantra: *Discipline your senses to purify your mind, body, and soul through your spiritual practice, nutritional behavior, physical fitness routine, and relationship with self and others.* Each archetype reveals how pain becomes power, chaos becomes clarity, and discipline becomes liberation.

Blending ancient and modern modalities, Orlen explores the tools of integration—non-attachment, letting go, faith, trust, meditation, prayer, surrender, and the intentional use of entheogens and regenerative medicine—as pathways toward balance and wholeness. Through deeply personal stories, he shares his own passage through pain, light, and surrender: *into the fire, through the fire, and becoming the fire.*

Integrating insights from the world's great faiths, philosophical systems, and spiritual sciences, *Higher Frequencies* offers both a roadmap and a mirror—an inquiry into how awareness, devotion, and vibration can purify the body, mind, and spirit toward higher states of consciousness.

More than a book, *Higher Frequencies* is a movement—a return to balance, authenticity, and resonance with the universal rhythm of life.

About the Author

Isaiah Sky Orlen is an entrepreneur, author, and visionary devoted to elevating human consciousness through wellness, community, and design. With two decades of experience leading brands across hospitality, spirits, gaming, and wellness—including leadership positions at Las Vegas Sands and Southern Glazer's Wine & Spirits—Isaiah brings a unique blend of executive insight, entrepreneurial creativity, and spiritual purpose to every endeavor.

Following his exit from the corporate arena, he launched CannaFAME in 2018, a global brand incubation company in the cannabis and alternative health sector, where he developed and scaled multiple consumer brands from concept to commercialization. He later founded a hemp brand incubator in 2020 and a regenerative medicine travel company in 2021, connecting individuals to mesenchymal stem cell treatments and integrative healing experiences in Colombia.

It was through a series of profound life challenges that Isaiah was called to explore the intersection between his business acumen, legal insight, and spiritual purpose. His journey began at Lehman Brothers, where his first day out of college was September 11, 2001—just hours before the planes came crashing into the towers. In September 2008, he started at Las Vegas Sands the very week the global financial crisis struck, marking one of the most turbulent periods in modern economic history. Years later, after two years of building the infrastructure, team, and brands under CannaFAME, its launch aligned with the onset of global COVID lockdowns. Through it all, Isaiah came to see these moments not as coincidence but as divine curriculum—an initiation into a deeper faith, trust, and alignment with higher consciousness that no traditional education could provide.

Today, Isaiah's core focus is the evolution of Higher Frequencies (HF)—a whole-life wellness and spiritual enlightenment platform rooted in ancient faiths and philosophies, the vibrational power of sound, and the discipline of the senses. Built upon the pillars of spiritual practice, nutritional behavior, physical fitness, and the relationship with self and others, HF serves as both a content ecosystem and a community network. Through its offerings and experiences, HF guides individuals and collectives alike in the purification of mind, body, and soul—supporting the journey toward balance, harmony, and enlightenment.

Through his book *Higher Frequencies: Journey to Enlightenment*, he invites readers to explore the path from awareness to mastery, and to vibrate at the frequency where personal evolution meets collective awakening.

A graduate of the University of Miami with a JD/MBA, Isaiah has been a member of the Florida Bar since 2006 and was a founding member of the Psychedelic Bar Association. His work continues to pioneer new ground in regenerative living, wellness travel, and the emerging spiritual economy—bridging commerce and consciousness to create systems that elevate human potential. Through initiatives spanning real estate, wellness, and experiential design, Isaiah's vision centers on building ecosystems that harmonize ancient wisdom with modern innovation, advancing a more conscious and connected world.

Part 1

Overview

Section 1 – Introduction to Isaiah and Higher Frequencies

Had I not walked the path I could not lead the way. Through Darkness comes light. Fire is a modality of light which burns away what no longer serves us and lights our soul with divine consciousness. It is through the difficulty we forge our divine self. Higher Frequencies is a journey through my own healing of my trauma, my health, and my mind. It is a study of the tools of spirituality, nutrition, and physical fitness that have aided me and continue to aid me on my journey. They have returned me to my breath and the realization that I am enough, that we are all G-D's children, and that we are all part of divine consciousness. There is no us or them, there is only we, and the sooner we learn this the sooner we return to the frequency of love and bring all those in this realm closer and closer to enlightenment. For we are all one divine frequency.

What does it mean to reach for Higher Frequencies? What is one's journey toward enlightenment all about? Is it about the elevation and purification of mind, body, and soul? Is it the understanding that you are a spirit having a human experience and that we are all part of one divine energy? Do you have the discipline to journey to enlightenment?

In this incarnation, I was born Jewish, which shapes my identity and my cultural, emotional, and spiritual compass. However, I also draw guidance from many other spiritualities and faiths: Yogic philosophy such as The Yoga Sutras of Patanjali, Kriya Yoga and Siddha Yoga, Stoicism, Christian mysticism, Chassidic thought, Jungian psychology, The Gene Keys, and the Map of Consciousness. Through my studies I have come to realize that the soul speaks a universal language, and truth wears many masks. Whether one calls it Hashem, Source, Brahman, Christ Consciousness, or simply Love—each path, when walked with sincerity, points toward the same light: union with the Divine.

My view is that religion is a tool for spiritual enlightenment. How the tool is used is ultimately up to the operator; tools can be used to manifest light and can be used to manifest darkness. Take a hammer, for example; it can be used to build a structure or as a weapon. In many instances, religion has been weaponized and is not being used for its intended purpose: to bring the mundane world to the spiritual realm.

The mundane realm refers to the physical, material world we experience through our senses and daily routines. The mundane world is linear, ego-based, governed by natural laws and logic, and prioritizes what can be seen, touched, and owned. It is a world built on duality and density, and is not necessarily bad.

The spiritual realm refers to the non-physical dimension of consciousness, where essence, presence, and higher frequencies reside. It includes non-linear time and space, unity of all beings and energies, higher frequencies informed by love, compassion, wisdom, and awareness, and subtle perception through intuition, inner knowing, divine guidance, and mystical experience. It can be accessed through prayer, meditation, revelation, or other elevated states of being.

Many spiritual paths and faiths teach that the goal is not to reject the mundane world, but to elevate it—to bring divine awareness into the material, and to live in the world while remaining connected to spirit. To be in it but not of it. We will arrive at this mantra throughout the book.

Religion shouldn't promote hatred toward another for their beliefs or their journey. And it shouldn't make you ashamed, fearful, or conjure up any other low frequency emotions. Rather, it should promote the love of oneself, the love of others, and give you questionable guidance on how to reach a more enlightened state. We shouldn't sit in judgement of another's journey or their tribe. We should celebrate each other's journey and tribes and look to the similarities that exist in ritual and tradition.

Higher Frequencies is not just a brand name I came up with; is the embodiment of my journey, my family's teachings, and all the many spiritual masters from various faiths and dialects that have helped illuminate my path. All things are based on energy, all things vibrate at a certain frequency, and our goal is to vibrate at higher frequencies with each day and with each interaction. And in doing so, we continue our journey to enlightenment, individually and collectively.

Higher Frequencies was born following a series of Ayahuasca ceremonies in Peru. I was in the process of exiting the alcohol space and entering the plant medicine arena. During the ceremony, I started to think about the intersection of my business and spiritual acumen, which seemed to be at odds with each other. That's when it hit me: my mission was to develop brands that were vehicles for change. Being that brands were demi-gods, we needed to infuse them with spirituality and teachings of well-being that would raise our vibration and the collective vibration of society.

Higher Frequencies was always meant to be a platform to help people on their journey to enlightenment and whole-life wellness. However, it initially started as a lifestyle company with products in the cannabis sector. The content and products were based on our families' spiritual teachings, the solfeggio frequencies, and chakras. Our cannabis products blended cannabinoids and botanicals associated with the frequencies & chakras to create seven distinct medicines. The content was focused on the healing benefits of the various spiritual practices, the frequencies, and the chakras, and it was centered around core social groups or tribes: spiritual enlightenment, wellness, travel, and music.

As they say, "man plans and G-D laughs." Three weeks before the hard launch, the country went into lockdown due to Covid. California was hit hard, and the cannabis market was hit even harder. There was no room for discovery of new brands as there were no consumer touch points. In an already difficult and nescient market, things got worse quickly, and we soon ran out of capital. I shelved the brands and the IP, and pivoted.

Over the next few years, I continued my business and personal journey, which became centered on spirituality, nutritional behavior, physical fitness, and my relationship with self and others. Through various modalities I began to shape myself into a new person. My faith and trust in the divine became unwavering, and Higher Frequencies began to take on new meaning.

Higher Frequencies was no longer about a product to me; it was a way of life. A compilation of my own journey and my own healing that I continue today. A whole-life wellness movement dedicated to elevating social consciousness and inspire health, connection, and enlightenment. Rooted in spiritual wisdom from diverse disciplines, its philosophy draws upon ancient practices, the elements of life, the vibrations of color and thought, the healing power of real foods, and the transformative power of music and sound.

The mission is to help individuals step into their power with courage, steadily moving toward the frequencies of love, transcendence, and enlightenment. And in doing so, to foster personal growth, evolve collective consciousness, and empower everyone to become their best selves, embrace love, and share it abundantly. BUT HOW CAN THIS BOOK, THIS PLATFORM, THIS MOVEMENT REALLY EFFECT CHANGE? It starts with the mantra and the tools for us all to take control of our own situation, to stop playing the victim and become the warrior no matter what life throws at us, no matter the set or setting. And to show up with equanimity, love, and light.

<u>Discipline your senses to purify your mind, body, and soul through your spiritual practice, nutritional behavior, physical fitness routine, and relationship with self and others.</u> This statement took me forty-five years to arrive at, and my hope is that through telling my story and the story of Higher Frequencies, I can aid others on their journey toward enlightenment.

Many people talk about concepts such as letting go, non-attachment, divinity, faith, and trust, but it is through integration of these concepts that one can elevate their consciousness and reach higher frequencies. One must be willing to practice discipline and walk through the fire of life. It is through this process that we are reminded we are all part of one divine consciousness.

It is irrelevant what modality of religion or spirituality one might lean upon to draw knowledge, strength, wisdom, and courage from, but rather the importance in recognizing the commonality, recognizing the frequency of love which permeates through all the great teachings. It is through this recognition that we can attune our frequency to that of love and move closer and closer to divine consciousness.

Throughout this book I am going to highlight some of the disciplines, spiritual teachings, and practices that have aided me on my journey toward enlightenment. My journey is an ongoing process, as it is a journey, not a destination. I will give examples on how I have applied these concepts to varied experiences in my life; sometimes as the victim, other times as the survivor, but always striving to become the warrior. I will discuss how I have integrated the lessons into my habits and behaviors.

We must remember that we are all on our own personal journey, and we must give ourselves grace to fall out of our discipline. It is okay to take a knee in life; the question is how long you are going to stay down. Are you going to play the victim card your whole life? Are you going to be the survivor and point to how much you've had to endure? Or are you going to rise in love and be the warrior? In each incarnation, we have a limited amount of time to heal, so you might as well get busy living.

It is through my journey that these lessons have gained meaning. My hope is my journey, and the personalization of these lessons, gives other members of our community a road map and assistance on their journey toward healing and enlightenment, and sparks curiosity to dig deeper into the studies of these concepts.

I have been blessed with a life filled with mentors and teachers in the spiritual and business world that many do not have access to or do not know where to find. It is my duty to share the lessons I have been gifted with all who will listen, to assist those that this resonates with on their journey with these transformative modalities, modalities that awaken the human connection to divine consciousness.

We must also understand that theories are meaningless unless we are willing to do the work necessary to integrate them into our lives so that they become habits and behaviors. This process can include a disassociation from people, places, things, and behaviors which no longer serve us. It can be isolating, lonely, and painful at times, but as they say, *'the burn is the blessing.'* You will come out the other side a newer stronger version of yourself. This will happen each time you make that conscious choice to walk in the fire of life and become the fire itself. Healing, growth, and spirituality are not destinations, they are a continuous journey. When one lesson is finished, another one begins; the path is not linear.

My hope is that through reading a bit about my story, you will see that I am not preaching from a position above the fire, but rather from within it. You have a choice in life: let the fire burn you, or let it transform you.

I will share tools that have helped me in my journey. I will add color to the conversation with personal stories and stories of those that I have aided in my journey. Please use this as a guide to see what may resonate, ask yourself questions, and do your own research.

Discipline is a word that many people feel is harsh. To some, it brings up emotions of negativity or restriction. I have thought about this often as Higher Frequencies, its philosophy, and my way of life are now based on the premise of discipline. One may think that using such a word would automatically turn many people off. I disagree, and I think we need to reframe the context and bring new light and love to the meaning of discipline.

It is understandable that many people view the word discipline through a distorted lens. As a child when the word was brought up it meant that we either did something wrong or we had new rules and regulations that were going to inhibit us from having a "good time." There is also a cultural view that through discipline we are denying ourselves of "something" rather than liberating ourselves.

As humans, we also tend to fear failure and discipline requires consistency. Many people feel that in order to live a disciplined life, they must be "perfect." This is not the case, as you must give yourself grace to fall out of your discipline. This is how we learn and come back stronger. Discipline is about getting uncomfortable for the sake of growth; it is an understanding that the burn is the blessing.

I want to challenge you to look at the word Discipline in a different light. What if you viewed this word as an act of devotion? A way of being that allows you to manifest the person you are meant to be rather than the avatar you are currently playing? A word that allows you to call into your life unlimited love and light? A word that allows you to liberate yourself from being a slave to your senses? Senses that have you constantly feeling like you are not enough, senses that have you constantly looking for external gratification, love and happiness? What if the word discipline allowed you to stop playing the victim and allowed you to become the warrior?

Discipline, in the context of Higher Frequencies, is a word that allows you to raise your vibration and learn to truly love yourself. It allows you to come to the realization that you are part of divine consciousness; so, you may love yourself unconditionally and share that love with all those you encounter without the want of reciprocity.

Discipline allows us to align our thoughts, actions, behaviors, and habits with the proper intentions, rather than allowing our senses to guide us from one desire to the next. When we allow our senses to control us, we live in chaos. We chase things that give us momentary pleasure and temporary satisfaction. Whether it be food, sex, alcohol, drugs, cars, watches, or relationships is irrelevant, as the feeling is external and fleeting, only to come to the realization that nothing external will ever bring us true happiness.

I want to be clear here: I am not saying don't enjoy life, nor am I saying that external pleasures and desires should be cut off completely. That is not realistic. After all, you are a spirit having a human experience, and you must partake in the experience to reconvene with the divine. Rather, it is necessary to practice Discipline and concepts such as non-attachment and letting go to maximize your time here in this incarnation. That is, if you want to be an active participant on your journey to enlightenment. Through our discipline, we raise our vibration and move in the direction of higher frequencies. We Rise in Love.

Section 2 – The Discipline Statement and Its Meaning

Discipline your senses to purify your mind, body, and soul through your spiritual practice, nutritional behavior, physical fitness routine, and relationship with self and others.

The above statement can be overwhelming; I'll be the first to admit that. I want to break it down a bit and make it a bit less daunting before diving into the archetypes of the Victim, the Survivor, and the Warrior and the tools and steps that can assist you on your journey to enlightenment.

Discipline of the Senses

The five senses, or as we may call them the sense telephones, send electrical stimuli to mind and body which creates our relationship with the world we live in, the mundane world. Our senses separate our physical body from our soul. Our physical body exists in this world, and is pivotal in our relationship with it, our health, and our daily lives. But we must not forget about our souls.

Our souls entered our physical body to have a human experience. And our ego would like us to be fully immersed in the human experience. In doing so, our ego speaks to us about desires, and through our senses, we fulfill these callings.

This becomes an impediment to our spiritual growth. While we need to recognize and live in this world, we also need to have an awareness that none of it is permanent. A term that is used in some spiritual faiths is Maya, the illusion or delusion. It is used to bring awareness that this world is illusionary or rather temporary, often referred to as 'mundane world.' Through our sense telephone we collect of impulses & frequencies. Our mind advises how we interpret and respond to them. If we do not practice discipline, we can get trapped in the illusion, attached to our ego, and stunt our spiritual growth. For some this may be okay, and while I don't like to make assumptions, my assumption is that if you are reading this book, that is not the case.

There are five traditional senses. Our sight or vision, which gives us the ability to perceive light, color shades, and depth. Our sense of hearing or audition, which gives us the perception of sound through our ears, including tone, rhythm, and vibration. Our sense of smell or olfaction, which detects the scent of particles in the air through the nose. Our sense of taste or gustation, which allows us to recognize and put definition to flavors through the taste buds, specifically sweet, sour, salty, butter, and umami. Last, our sense of touch or tactile sense, which allows us to feel pressure, temperature, texture, and pain through the skin and body.

These senses are not just physical tools; they also are gateways that influence our energetic and emotional states. Through them we can raise or lower our vibration. All aspects of the universe carry frequencies. When we interreact with food, people, and environments, our senses bring these frequencies into our physical, emotional, and spiritual being. Negative attracts negative or low frequencies, and positive attracts positive or high frequencies. Without discipline, one ends up following their desires and various emotional states. This opens you up to energies that do not serve your highest purpose.

Our senses create our reality; they are integral to how our body interacts with our mind. They affect how we think about ourselves, our environment, and others. Without discipline, our desires become the masters of such activities as eating, thinking, listening, seeing, and speaking. When this occurs, we lose control of our sense of divinity, become entangled in our ego, and remain in low frequency states of being.

Purification of your Mind, Body, and Soul

By controlling our five senses, we can purify the three aspects of our physical, emotional, and spiritual being: the mind, the body, and the soul. Without discipline of the senses, our mind, body, and soul become polluted with negative stimuli from food, sounds, sights, smells, and physical touch points. With discipline, we can actively purify the mind, body, and soul, allowing us to raise our vibration in the material and spiritual realms.

The body is our physical vessel. It is composed of matter and governed by nature and time. Our physical body uses its five senses to interact with the material world in which inputs and actions can create joy, pain, and a spectrum of emotions in between. Our spiritual body is a temple or channel for divine consciousness and energy; through prayer and meditation, we can channel the spiritual body into the physical body. Through this purification process, we can alleviate pain, suffering, anxiety, and trauma.

Our body is a sacred vessel that was created in the physical world to be elevated to the spiritual world. Therefore, it is impermanent, and is a vehicle to work through energies that do not serve our soul. This is a part of the purification process. Some believe that our physical body is a vessel to work through our karma, karma being past wrongs we have committed or unfulfilled obligations from previous incarnations. Our body keeps us connected to the illusion or delusionary state of this physical world, or Maya.

It is through our body that our frequency is expressed. Whether we are vibrating at low or high frequencies is dependent on our habits and behaviors; do they purify or do they pollute you?

For example, you can either contract in fear or expand in love, and this can be seen by those you encounter through your body language. We must treat the body as sacred vessel. Through our purification and discipline, we cleanse, nourish, rest, and strengthen our body during its physical journey in the material world.

The mind is tied to our ego. It is what connects us to this material and mundane world and shapes our reality through our thoughts, perception, and memory. Our mind processes our emotions, thoughts, judgments, and reactions. To access higher frequencies, we must lead a disciplined life so we can actively purify any thoughts that create negative or limiting beliefs. Without discipline, your mind can be your worst enemy, and with discipline, your mind could be your best friend.

Our mind is both intellectual and emotional, which can lead to both ignorance and liberation. This is highly dependent on what modalities we use to discipline and purify our thinking. At its lowest frequency, it lives in the negative and allows desires and ego to control its narrative. However, at higher frequencies, its narrative is one of divine faith and trust, and it understands its connectivity and oneness with divine consciousness. It is our mind that aligns us with our frequencies. Without care and purification, we remain in low vibratory states of being.

The soul is our connection to divine consciousness, for it is divine consciousness. Our soul has lived through many incarnations but remains untouched by them. It merely breathes life into the physical form. It is our souls' mission to reconvene with divine consciousness; however, it must live out its lifetimes to fulfill its mission in the physical form and work through its karma, negative baggage, before doing so.

Our soul is a literal piece of divine consciousness, and when our body and mind are purified, we can listen to the communication of the universe through our soul. It is our eternal flame that remains burning during many lifetimes and vibrates at the highest frequencies, the frequency of enlightenment. It is the divine light within.

The soul exists beyond time and space and is in constant communication with divine consciousness. However, when we allow low frequencies to enter the body and mind, the souls' line of communication becomes distorted and damaged. It is through the process of purification that we cleanse the energy channels and strengthen our connection in the physical form with divine consciousness.

Through the purification of the mind, body, and soul, we connect to divine consciousness, move toward higher frequencies, and come closer and closer to enlightenment. While enlightenment cannot be reached in the material world, we can lay the groundwork through purification for the day we transition.

The final aspect to our mental, physical, spiritual, and emotional well-being is the modalities centered around spirituality, physical fitness, nutritional behavior, our relationship with self and others, and how we incorporate them into our daily behaviors. These modalities are practiced or applied to aid in our discipline. In doing so, they assist us in purifying our mind, body, and soul. They are the core aspects in our journey to enlightenment as they are the actions or inactions taken to heal.

Spiritual Practice

The foundation of one's spiritual practice can encompass several things such as prayer, meditation, yoga, attending houses of worship, reading books, using ancestral medicine, breathwork, wellness retreats, and even listening to various forms of media and shows. The books one incorporates into their spiritual practice may be religious texts or scripture, books on self-improvement, or books on the journeys of others who have walked the path, such as this one.

While certain aspects of the spiritual practice may happen irregularly, such as sitting in a medicine ceremony or attending a breathwork or yoga retreat, it is imperative to have a daily spiritual practice. For example, many people and faiths find it helpful to have a segmented amount of time in the morning and evening to meditate and/or pray. This allows one to start and end the day with a clear and calm mind. It also opens us up to communicate with divine consciousness, asking for any assistance personally or for loved ones that may need it. It may be as simple as meditating for twenty minutes and adding some prayers for your loved ones and those in need in the world.

You may also consider joining a prayer or mediation group. This isn't necessarily a religious group. Rather, it may be a spiritual group that meets a few times a week to meditate. It may be your local yoga studio or wellness studio where you find your tribe to flow and find your breath.

Sharing your time, kindness, and love without the want of reciprocity is another form of spiritual practice. Giving of yourself to aid others in their healing and journey to enlightenment with no expectation is spirituality in its purest form.

Your spiritual practice should return you to your breath, your life force. It is through our breath that we reconnect to divine consciousness. It is through our breath we have an awareness that our physical body is merely a vehicle for our spiritual soul. It is through our spiritual practice we find our breath, calm our mindchatter, align our frequencies, and live a disciplined life which aids us in our journey to enlightenment.

Nutritional Behavior

As the saying goes, you are what you eat. You should eat what is real. Some questions to ask: was it processed? Is it living food? Would your grandparents recognize it? Food has both an effect on our physical and mental well-being. Our food carries the energy and nourishment our body needs. But todays foodie culture and fast living can have us making poor choices, choices based on pleasures and desires rather than on health.

Poor food choices can lead to all sorts of health issues such as cardiovascular disease, diabetes, obesity; the list is endless. These choices can also leave us feeling lethargic. Why is this? Food carries energy. I am not merely talking about calories, but also the energy of how it was manufactured and processed, and how it arrived at your plate.

Traditionally, we ate regionally, and we ate foods that we picked from the earth or hunted from the land, air, or sea. However, as we moved into larger cities and started more of a fast-paced life, our food supply chain changed. Food became processed items, traveled long distances, and were not sourced regionally. People are finally taking notice that these ultra-processed foods are harmful to one's physical, mental, and emotional state.

Everyone needs to find what works for their nutritional behavior and eat the food which they align with ethically, emotionally, spiritually, and physically. Whether one wants to label themselves a carnivore, vegan, vegetarian, pescatarian, or omnivore comes down to several factors that can be both personal and health-related.

No matter your label, you must recognize that what we put in our body has a dramatic effect on our overall well-being. We should all try to return to a living diet, whether plant based and/or animal based, where the ingredients can be traced to origin and were not by way of a science experiment in a lab. Staying away from ingredients that did not originate in the soil, land, or sea is always a good idea. It is also helpful to eat food sourced within your geography, when possible. This ensures the least touch points and points of contamination.

Nutritional behavior is something that is very personal. Judging or shaming someone for their food choices doesn't benefit the community. Food can be healing or harming. And it is up to the individual to make the choices they are in alignment with; however, there are some things these days being marketed as nourishment that are chemically addictive and that poison the body rather than nourish the body. Do not let your desires guide your nutritional behavior.

Physical Fitness Routine

Your physical fitness routine helps not only your physical health, but also your mental health and well-being. Through your physical fitness routine, you not only keep your physical body in shape, but you also return to your breath, your life force. Many people call this state of being the flow state.

When you enter the flow state through physical fitness, the noise of the outside world becomes muted. You can connect to your inner voice, divinity, in a manner that allows you to process emotions that are no longer serving you. In this manner physical fitness is a moving meditation. It helps to discipline all our senses.

It doesn't matter how you move your body, just move it and move it regularly. Whether it is walking, running, biking, high-intensity interval training (HIIT), yoga, pilates, swimming, or any other modality, it is important for your spiritual, mental, physical, and emotional health to have a regular routine. Without a regular physical fitness routine, one is prone to make excuses before ever acting.

It also helps to find something you enjoy doing, so you look forward to it rather than dread it. We all have different likes. Our bodies all function differently, and we all live in different environments, so you need to find the modality that works for you. Whether it be in a class, a gym, or outside makes no difference; you just need to show up and flow.

Relationship with Self and Others

How we see, listen, speak, and think about ourselves and to others has a direct impact on the vibrational state of our being and our interactions themselves. We must discipline our senses to ensure we have a positive relationship with ourselves and others, as this has a direct impact on the purity of our mind and soul. It can also have an impact on our body; many doctors now believe that physical ailments start with trauma in the mind. These negative impressions on the mind, otherwise known as traumas, cause inflammatory effects on our body and in turn can trigger all sorts of physical health issues.

If we only see, listen, speak, and think in a negative manner about ourselves and others, then we are calling in low frequencies. We are coloring all our interactions with negative emotions. Many people get trapped in their own trauma and negative dialogue and wonder why more of the same shows up in their life.

But the reverse is true as well; we can call in higher frequencies if we focus on a positive relationship with self and others that is drenched in light, love, hope, and continued blessings. When we catch ourselves viewing and listening to life through a negative lens, we can take corrective actions through prayer, meditation, conversation with loved ones, or even just going for a walk to reframe our perspective.

Treating yourself and others with kindness can be one of the most difficult aspects of the human experience. Our ego and the emotions such as jealousy, shame, anxiety, and fear play a major part in harming our relationship with self and others. Through our disciplines we can silence the noise of these bad actors, and we can have a positive outlook and view on all aspects of who we are and who we interact with, which in turn will bring healing and love to all these interactions.

Take one bite of the apple at a time. And as mentioned, and will be mentioned again and again, give yourself grace to fall out of your discipline. It can take months to turn new behaviors into habits. If you try to modify too many things at once, you may crash and burn and become discouraged by your progress. Best to choose a behavior, modify it, turn it into a habit, and move on to the next; you have at least this lifetime to get it right, and probably a few more.

Part 2

The Archetypal Path: Victim/Survivor/Warrior

We must make choices in life. We must choose how we act and how we react. We can allow life to have a detrimental effect on our frequencies, or we can view all things as neither negative nor positive but lessons that are a part of our spiritual, physical, and emotional growth. We can move through life unbalanced, or we can move through life with equanimity. It's your choice to decide what part you want to play. Do you want to be the victim, do you want to be the survivor, or do you want to be the warrior?

I say without shame that I've lived through the Victim, I've survived the Survivor, and I now strive each day to embody the Warrior. The journey through these archetypes is not neat or linear. You must push through pain, suffering, and limiting beliefs. There are times in my life were I "take a knee" and allow my mindstuff or ego promote the victim or the survivor. Through my self-discipline, I regain control of my senses, turn within, and remind myself it is about sitting in the fire rather than avoiding it.

Mindstuff, also referred to as Chitta in Kriya Yoga, is the total field of consciousness that records impressions, thoughts, memories, desires, and perceptions. It shapes our reality and can have us lost in the illusionary world. Mindstuff is the medium through which our prana or life-force flows. When we are restless, distracted, anxious, or fearful, it flows outward, which leads to distraction and bondage to our senses. However, we can purify our mindstuff when we discipline our senses and gain control of our breath, drawing our prana inward and upward toward our connection to divine consciousness.

This is what some call doing the work or integrating, which can be a disassociation from habits, people, places, and things that do not serve your higher self, which at times can be isolating and lonely. Through it, we realize that the burn is the blessing, and the fire of life burns off what no longer services you. Eventually, you realize you are the fire, and no harm can come to you as you are divinely protected. You are divine consciousness manifested in the physical form.

You must face life with equanimity and be the peaceful warrior. You must show up with persistence, perseverance, and patience. You must give yourself the grace to fall out of your discipline. But if you stay the course, you will grow spiritually, emotionally, & physically as you journey closer to self-realization and enlightenment.

Equanimity is one's ability to remain in a state of mental calm, composure, and even temper, no matter what obstacles of life may present themselves. Whether the ocean of life is mellow or a storm is brewing, equanimity allows one to remain still and removes emotional instability from decisions and reactions to life.

Through the practice of equanimity, one finds emotional stability, which aids in stress, fear, and anxiety reduction. Equanimity improves relationships as it promotes clear and calm communication and allows one to listen more intuitively rather than respond and react. It aids with clarity of mind, spiritual growth, resilience, and adaptability. Equanimity not only helps the mind calm, but also leads to improved physical health, lowering one's stress and calming one's nervous system. Many great faiths and philosophies such as stoicism are based in the practice of equanimity.

The journey to spiritual enlightenment is a layered evolution through archetypes that reflect one's relationship with pain, identity, and divine purpose. On my journey toward enlightenment, I have come to the realization that there are three foundational archetypes—*the Victim, the Survivor, and the Warrior*—each representing a distinct stage of awakening and self-realization. These archetypes can also be applied to various situations that life presents us depending on the set and setting. Let's put some definition to the archetypes and then see how they might affect the interaction of our journey and our discipline.

The Victim

The Victim lives in the shadow and pain of their past experiences. They are unable to let go and constantly relive trauma, adding unnecessary pain and suffering to the present. They revisit their traumas and injustices, both internally and externally, allowing these experiences to shape their identity and dominate their emotional, mental, and physical state.

The Victim resists surrender, clings to blame, and struggles to release attachments that keep them connected to further pain and suffering. They are incapable of practicing letting go and would rather live in the past and in their negative emotions. Their mindset is rooted in fear, anxiety, and separation, which impedes their ability to trust in a higher power. This chronic state of inner conflict prevents the flow of healing and elevates neither their frequency nor their consciousness. The Victim's journey is clouded by the illusion of powerlessness; they feel they have no control over the life they are living.

I played the victim in some instances earlier in life. This was in part due to both personal and generational trauma. The pain was shown externally through my interactions with others and myself. Playing the victim caused me to have full-body anxiety attacks and limiting beliefs that were coupled with thoughts of shame, blame, and fear. My nervous system was constantly in flux, depending on the issue that was most prevalent of the day.

I meditated, worked out, and prayed, but I lacked the faith and trust that I now have in divine consciousness. The physical tightness of my muscles was a direct result of my inability to surrender to life. The Victim archetype clings to suffering because it fears the unknown more than it despises its pain. In spiritual terms, this is the state of avidya—ignorance of one's true nature.

The Survivor

The Survivor has taken steps beyond victimhood but remains tethered to their past. They constantly reference all they have been through as a proving ground of how far they have come.

However, in doings so, they still identify with their pain and suffering and use it to define who they are to others. It is part their identity and conjures up negative energy and negative emotions associated with the experiences of the past.

When interacting with others, they wear their trauma as a badge of honor or justification for current limitations. Survivors often externalize their lack of progress, blaming circumstances, their past, or others for why their life isn't manifesting as desired.

They lean into relationships where they find temporary comfort in the shared language of suffering and remain anchored in ego-based narratives. While more empowered than the Victim, the Survivor is still influenced by unresolved negative energies and low frequencies. Their growth is stunted by the inability to fully release the past, live in the present, and practice gratitude for the lesson generated from the past traumas or circumstances.

In playing the survivor, I still identified with my past wounds and trauma. I felt I needed to share them to justify where I was currently at in my journey toward enlightenment, both personally and spiritually. In many aspects of my life, I had a survivor's mentality. This archetype wears trauma like armor: proud, resilient, but still tethered to the past. Survivors often plateau because they believe healing is synonymous with control. We achieve just enough spiritual awareness to say, "I'm not who I used to be," but not enough to become who we are meant to be.

And then there comes a point in our lives, in our spiritual journey, when we no longer want to live on our knees. When we realize that the person that is hurting us the most is ourselves, someone conjured up by our own mind. I began to search out various modalities of healing on my terms. I began to forge new habits in my spiritual, physical, and nutritional behavior which quieted my mindstuff and calmed my nervous system. I realized that there was no one to blame but myself for how I felt, where I was at in life, or where I was going. In walks the warrior.

The Warrior

The Warrior, in contrast, embodies spiritual discipline, divine faith and trust, conscious non-attachment, and proactively practices letting go. They practice equanimity and have a stoic demeanor in all aspects and interactions in life. The warrior surrenders to life and takes the seat of the witness; letting go of things that no longer serve them on their journey toward enlightenment.

This archetype transmutes pain into power by recognizing trauma as a sacred teacher—not a defining identity. The Warrior walks the path of enlightenment through practicing discipline, mastering the senses, cultivating inner stillness, and aligning with divine consciousness. They have arrived at the understanding that negative emotions and low frequencies are impermanent expressions within the field of consciousness, and they seek to rise above these energetic attractor fields through their spiritual practice, physical fitness routine, nutritional behavior, and relationships with self and others. In doing so, they purify their mind, body, and soul, raise their vibration, and call in higher frequencies.

Warriors do not suppress their past but integrate it as part of their soul's correction across lifetimes. They understand that there is no positive and negative, but rather only lessons to be learned on their journey to enlightenment. They are battle-born—luminous carriers of divine consciousness whose mission is to awaken themselves and others. The Warrior no longer reacts to life, but responds with grace, wisdom, and a commitment to serve as a vessel for healing, light, and love.

The Warrior lives on the other side of surrender. They have alchemized their wounds into their strength, letting go of things that no longer serve them on their journey, whether it be emotions, thoughts, habits, or people. They know the difference between non-attachment and detachment. This is the individual who lives in alignment with divine will—where prayer, breath, movement, and service become one seamless expression of love in alignment with divine consciousness.

They are the light. They are on the road to self-realization knowing that one's true nature is beyond the ego, the body, and the mind. It is the understanding that you are a soul having a human experience in this world; you are not your personality, your thoughts, or your emotions. You are divine consciousness.

Ideally, I would like to be the warrior at all points and in all circumstances in my life, and while I walk with this intention, I am still a soul having a human experience, and I am far from perfect. There are days and happenings where I oscillate between the warrior and the survivor, but I have an awareness that allows me to fall back into my discipline, give myself a moment of grace, and rise in love to the warrior.

I find guidance in walking the path of the warrior through my spiritual practice, my physical fitness routines, and my nutritional behavior. Through a disciplined life, I embody and become the warrior. The warrior engages the world not to gain validation, but to be a vessel for healing and transformation, including for oneself. Each day is a new day to burn off something that is no longer serving us and to grow into a stronger version of ourselves through our discipline.

My hope is to align with the lineage of my ancestors and other indigenous leaders and always cultivate a warrior mentality. I commit to do this through my spiritual and physical practice, in my prayer and meditation, and in my fallings and risings. I strive to be a vessel for light and love. I turn within to cultivate the energy of divine love and divine consciousness, and I share this energy without the want of reciprocity, unconditionally. And every day, I recommit even when I stumble and need to take a knee. To me, that is being and becoming the warrior archetype.

In essence, spiritual enlightenment unfolds through the alchemy of these archetypes: from the disempowerment of the Victim, to the self-awareness of the Survivor, to the divine embodiment of the Warrior. Only through the Warrior's path can one transcend ego, release the chains of suffering, and vibrate in harmony with higher frequencies of truth, unity, love and light. You must burn and disassociate habits, behaviors, places, people, and things that no longer serve you. The warrior sits in the fire of life, and through this suffering becomes enlightened. The warrior becomes the light.

My Journey Through the Archetypes

It is easy to say be the warrior, but how do you become the warrior? How do you step into your strength, courage and power? Through the application of our mantra, discipline your senses to purify your mind, body, and soul through your spiritual practice, nutritional behavior, physical fitness routine, and relationship with self and others, I was able to move from the Victim to the Survivor to the Warrior. Let me highlight this using my experience surviving 9/11/01 and my interactions with both business and personal relationship.

When I arrived at the North Tower on September 11, 2001, I was dressed in a new designer suit, wing tip shoes, and was ready to make my entrance to Wall Street. I had a secured a job right out of college for Lehman Brothers. At the time, they were the largest fixed income financial institution on Wall Street.

Growing up in Staten Island, I used to take the Ferry to the city regularly in high school. I loved New York and what it stood for. New York to me wasn't a "melting pot;" rather, it was a mixed salad. I say a mixed salad because the various immigrant cultures all retained their identity but also functioned as one. It felt like a dream to be walking into buildings that I used to stare at in awe. And now I was beginning my career here, in the financial epicenter of the world.

My first meeting was on the 39th Floor of 3 World Financial, and the COO of the Lehman was welcoming our group into the fall operations analyst program. All of a sudden, we heard a loud boom. Upon opening the blinds to the conference room, we saw the unthinkable; a gapping whole and fire shooting out of the North Tower across the street and twenty floors above us.

The Port Authority came on the intercoms in the building and told us not to evacuate, as there was an "accident" they were assessing. I immediately thought this to be a terrorist attack, but it all felt surreal. I made my way to a payphone on the floor, as there was no cell service, and called my sister in Florida. My family was frantic, as they didn't know what building I was in. While I was speaking to her, I heard screams. It was a that moment the second plane hit the South Tower.

I told my sister I loved her, hung up, and made my way to the staircase. We now knew we were under attack, and it was time to get out. I remember thinking that the planes hit higher up, so each time I descended a few flights I felt a bit safer. I was clearly in a state of shock as I moved through the experiences of that day and the weeks to come.

The next few hours were chaotic, to say the least. It was hard to put into words the amount of death, destruction, confusion, fear, and anger I saw and felt as I walked out into the World Trade Center Plaza that morning. It seemed like a scene out of a Hollywood movie, except I was in New York, and it wasn't a movie.

I made it a few blocks away when I stopped with a colleague to try to use a pay phone. And then it happened. The ground started shaking, we looked up, and the first tower was collapsing. Everyone just ran. Fortunately, the dust cloud missed me by about a block.

The next few hours, days, and months were full of trauma. There is no way to mentally prepare yourself for living in the uncertainty that was New York that fall. The pile burned on, bomb threats were common, fighter jets were overhead patrolling, and there was a constant pitch of the sirens of emergency vehicles. I'd walk outside of my apartment building on 34th and Park and be confronted with the smell of the burning pile, the national guard with M-16's in hand, and missing posters lining the streets and subways of those who would never return home to their loved ones.

When I was asked by friends and family how I was doing, I would just say, you can take a knee but there is no point in sitting in a corner and crying. My grandfather lost many family members during the Holocaust and served in WWII, and he still got up every morning, raised a family, and ran a fruit store in Brooklyn. To me, it would have been a dishonor to his memory to not face this crisis head on and keep moving forward.

For years I played the Survivor, telling my story to those who asked and wearing my trauma as a badge of honor. The experience had a dramatic effect on my behavior and choices in the coming decades. I decided to go to Law School and get my MBA, but something was off. I didn't fully commit to anything; I got my degrees and passed my bar but didn't commit to the field. I didn't commit to relationships; I would start something and then move on to the next deal or experience the minute I got bored or uncomfortable.

When it came to my drinking, eating, and partying, I was bringing new meaning to the word bacchanal. It wasn't until I decided to sit with Ayahuasca, which was about fifteen years after 9/11/01, that I came to terms with what happened that day and the fact that I never stopped running, just like I ran down the stairs and away from the Towers on that day. Running from myself, running from commitment, running from pain, running from anything that was going to tie me down, bring me discomfort, or have me stop running.

In ceremony, I was reminded that I am the warrior. It was time to take off the masks that I put on during 9/11 and the following years. The masks I used to hide my scars were no longer serving me on my journey toward enlightenment. All that I had gone through was meant to be; my lessons in life made me, including this day, and were molding me into the healer and warrior I am today.

But first I had to heal myself. The warrior gets injured, the warrior goes through hardships, but rather than wearing them as a badge, the warrior gains the knowledge of the lessons and looks to grow personally and professionally and helps others grow collectively from the lesson that have learnt.

Whether it is a lover, business partner, a family member, or just a friend, our relationships with others can have dramatic, traumatic, or healing effects on our relationship with ourselves. Many times, we fail to see others' points of view or are clouded by the occurrences of our past experiences. This can lead us to playing the victim in our relationships. And sometimes we remain in an abusive situation due to false scenarios we construct in our head or possibly just so we can get even when the tide turns.

In any case, we must practice discipline of listening, speaking, and thinking in our personal and business relationships to rise to the warrior in all our interactions. We will turn to these maxims and how to do so later in the book and go over their meaning and their application.

One must remember a warrior is not always in battle. A warrior does not always need to lead with the sword or arrive with a fiery disposition. There is the concept of the peaceful warrior. The one who can dissect the situation, learn from it, and not allow it to cause any additional physical, emotional, or spiritual harm to those involved. The peaceful warrior is focused on resolution, not destruction.

A few years back I had a dear friend ask me to commit to a loan deal with him. I had known him for years. He had been to dinner with my family, and I even had the security codes to his house. I knew his business dealings as well and had confirmed several successful deals he had done. I explained to him that my cash flow wasn't in a healthy spot, but that I would support him in any manner I could.

We executed all necessary paperwork, and I was to receive the principal and the interest back in four months. About three months in, I received a call from the borrower stating he had never received the funds and that my friend had defrauded him, others, and most likely me. As a good friend does, I assured the borrower this wasn't the case, but as soon as I started to dig in, the web of lies and deceit became apparent.

At first, I felt like a victim. I took a woe-is-me attitude. How could someone I loved and considered family defraud me of something so trivial as money? How could I let this happen? What could I have done differently? My "friend" kept assuring me he was going to make it right. We had many conversations, and I continued to act like a victim, allowing my abuser to continue in his ways.

Finally, I said enough. We drafted a legal agreement that assured me the return of my money on a certain date. While he had not kept his word for months, I clung to the belief that he would now that there was a legal document.

Throughout this time, I lost sleep and allowed negative energies and thoughts to consume my mind and my time. Hey, but at least I had survived the experience, and I had been victorious over his deceit and lies. He made the initial payment, but then crickets. All additional payments ceased as well as his communication.

As they say sometimes, the juice isn't worth the squeeze. I had to make a choice: fall back into a victim mentality, feel like I survived the experience, or become the warrior, as this wasn't the first time and wouldn't be the last time that a friends' mask would come off in a business deal and there would be a demon behind it.

The problem with the victim and survivor mentality is that you hold on to things that harm you and you remain attached to people and emotions that no longer belong in your life. You fail to practice non-attachment and letting go, which are primary tools for your journey to enlightenment. This creates further emotional and spiritual harm to your psyche. We will dive deeper into these concepts further in the book. Let's get back to my friend the thief, or rather should I say, my friend the angel who was a lesson sent by the divine to teach me I am the warrior.

I say this because through the pain of this experience, I learned how to be a warrior. I learned that holding onto anger, wanting to get even, or wanting to prove a point only dulls my frequency and keeps me in a victim or survivor state of mind. It only further attracts lower frequencies. Nothing is ever gained by force. You must step into power and rise above these situations.

By letting go, practicing non-attachment, and saying a blessing for those that have wronged me, I became the peaceful warrior. I chose light over darkness. I chose to be a better friend to myself and to not allow others' actions to cause me mental, emotional, or spiritual harm. I learned that there are going to be times when people you love wrong you, but that doesn't have to affect you and you don't have to beat yourself up with the negative self-talk of should've, could've, or would've. Rather, you must look at what you might have once perceived as a negative situation and turn it into positive light, and respond with love rather than anger. Through this we remain the warrior, the peaceful warrior, the warrior of light and love. And in doing so, we invite in higher frequencies.

Part 3

Discipline

Overview

Discipline your senses to purify your mind, body, and soul through your spiritual practice, nutritional behavior, physical fitness routine, and relationship with self and others.

Discipline is a word that most people do not like to hear, as it can illicit feelings of restriction and punishment. However, through discipline we can find ourselves on the road to liberation and self-realization. It allows us to have total freedom, go beyond our limitations, and break through boundaries we thought were insurmountable.

We are specifically speaking of the discipline of our controlling our senses and the illusions they create. In a world where one can have sensory overload through our smart phones, digital billboards, and other media, one must be discerning of what they allow to shape their reality. What we take in via our senses will have a direct impact on our overall health as it relates to the purity of mind, body, and soul.

When we lack discipline in our senses, we invite in all sorts of energies that do not serve us. These energies lead to exhaustion, dejection, anxiety, depression, contempt, cynicism, fear, shame, and a myriad of other emotions and health issues that keep us from living our best life. They create limiting beliefs that do not allow us to maximize our spiritual, physical, and emotional potential, and keep us trapped in a spectrum of lower frequencies.

It is of utmost importance to control your senses and forgo momentary pleasures and desires, which can lead to negative emotions and misinterpretations. In our pursuit of love and understanding, one must practice discipline. Love and understanding of ourselves and others.

Discipline of the Senses is a core tenant to living a spiritual life. It is expanded upon in many of the great faiths and religions of the world. Our sense telephones create our relationship with the external world around us. It is through theses sense telephones that electricities send messages to our mind and body, shaping how we interact with our environment, electricities being the energy transmuted throughout the physical body by the nerve.

The optic nerve carries light and allows one to perceive light color, shapes, and movement through the eyes. The auditory nerve carries sound, hearing, and detects sound through vibrations in the ear. The olfactory nerve carries smell, sensing odors through the nose. The trigeminal nerve carries touch, feeling pressure, temperature, pain, and texture through the skin, especially from the face. And the glossopharyngeal nerve carries taste, sending flavors through the tongue: sweet, sour, salty, bitter, and umami. These are the "sense messengers" that allow the soul, through the body, to interact with the material world—each with its own frequency and corresponding discipline on the path to higher consciousness and higher frequencies.

If we do not practice discipline of the senses, we fall victim to the illusion of the world around us. It is the mind, more specifically the ego, that can cause this to happen. We fall into a state of maya, delusion, or trance and move further away from our goal of witness consciousness, or rather divine consciousness. We let our desires lead us on an endless quest of momentary happiness, but we never reach enlightenment or bliss.

Another way we can look at the sense telephones is as the cities or gates of the body. The gates being the ears, eyes, nose, mouth and hands/skin. It is through these gates that stimuli from the external world or mundane world enters our personal world, our bodies, and our spiritual realm. In an interpretation Old Testament, there is in analogy between physical cities and our physical bodies; in physical cities we station judges and sheriffs to prevent crime, and similarly we must do the same at the gates to our physical body. We station these "judges and sheriffs" or "disciplines" at our sense gates to prevent stimuli from entering our physical and mental body that could be detrimental to our spiritual well-being.

When we lack discipline of our senses, our spiritual growth is stunted, and we are detoured on our journey to enlightenment and from reaching higher frequencies. We forget that our souls' purpose for being here is to uplift the mundane world to the spiritual world, infusing ordinary life with divine light, meaning, love, and consciousness, to arrive at the conclusion that there is no separation and that we are all one divine energy, divine consciousness. That is why we must practice discipline of the senses.

1. Discipline your senses through your Spiritual Practice

    a) Discipline in Silence

        i. Discipline in silence is the practice of turning off our senses and connection to the outside world and stimuli. We can connect to the source by turning within and silencing our "sense telephones." This is a major key, as through the silencing of our senses we can turn within and directly connect to the source, as we are all one. One path to silence is through meditation. There are various ways one can meditate to achieve inner silence. The goal is to align one's energy with the universe and receive divine messages through the silence. It can be detachment from physical action, talking, and from thinking with the goal of experiencing self to connect to the higher power. But it can also be achieving a flow state through physical action, where one is present in the activity, but the mind becomes silenced through our cadenced breathing.

    b) Discipline in Thinking and Contemplation

        i. Our constant companion on our journey is our mind. It is what keeps us rooted in the reality of this world. And no one controls it but you. Until it has become completely connected to the source and detached from ego, it is there as part of the human experience. Having discipline in thinking and the stories you tell yourself is of utmost importance on your spiritual path. Your mind shapes your view of who you are and the energy you project and walk with. Thinking is how we process thought through analyzation, comparison, solving problems, and planning. Contemplation is more intentional and is inwardly focused. Where thinking is reactionary to the sense telephones taking in stimuli, contemplation is a pause, a pause before a pivot.

2. Discipline your senses through your Nutritional Behavior

a) The food we take in can be medicine or it can be poison. This is with respect to the nutritional value, how it was procured, and the amount we consume. There is a lot to unpack here, as referred to the nutritional content of what we eat as well as the frequency of food we consume. Frequency being how much we consume as well as the frequency or energy of the food itself.

It is no secret that food carries energy. Its primary purpose is to provide CALORIES, and it gives us the life force we need to carry on in our human form. Processed foods and other harmful addictive ingredients have become commonplace in most diets, as has overeating due to generational fear and trauma which has led to a scarcity mindset in many. A scarcity mindset is the belief that you will never have enough, so you must take in as much as you can when you can.

These are all harmful behaviors to raising your vibration and our physical and mental well-being, behaviors that can pollute rather than purify the mind and body. When we can, we should try to eat living foods and focus on eating to the point just before we are full which aids in the purification process and keeps us rooted in our discipline.

3. Discipline your senses through your Physical Fitness Routine

   a) Your physical fitness routine is a major key into the discipline of your senses and ultimately the purification of your mind, body, and soul. Physical Fitness keeps one's body in optimal working condition, is an excellent stress and anxiety release, and reconnects one to their breath. Through physical fitness, one can refine their sensory inputs and motor outputs that shape our mental clarity, emotional stability, and spiritual alignment. Your physical fitness routine is the front lines of your setting up for the purification of your body and mind.

4. Discipline your senses through your Relationship with Self and Others

   a) Discipline Your Eyes: How You see Yourself and Others

      i. To have clarity in the picture you are visually creating about yourself and the environment you exist in, one must choose the imagery their eyes perceive. One must be discerning of what types of images and the energy those images carry they allow into their sight. We want to make sure we are taking in images that carry the light of divine consciousness. You must have a positive outlook on how you physically view yourself, and it is imperative to be careful on how you communicate your energy which comes through your eyes. One must be aware of their gaze and what it is saying to those they interact with. Your eyes have a direct impact on attracting low or high frequency energies, as what you see is what will become reality, creating the set and setting of the world YOU live in.

b) Discipline Your Ears: How You Listen to Yourself and Others

   i. What you listen to carries with it not only messages but also vibrations on certain frequencies. If you are not discerning, you may be subject to listening to negative frequencies and messages, which in turn will lower your frequencies, putting you in lower states of consciousness.

     You also want to be receptive and open to those who are communicating with you. This means being respectful and giving someone your undivided attention when they are speaking to you. Remember they have taken time to share their energy with you, and you should not be distracted by things such as your phone, social media, or the thoughts in your head while interacting with others.

c) Discipline Your Mouth: How You Speak to Yourself and Others

   i. Both of the statements "The Power of the Spoken Word" and "Your Word is Your Wand" imply that what you speak into the universe becomes your reality as the universe is listening. We can speak things into existence, so we must take extra care in what we say to others and how we speak to ourselves. If we are projecting and speaking negatively, then we shouldn't be shocked when life doesn't go our way and negative events unfold. If we have this understanding, then why wouldn't we be kind in the things we say to others and kind in the things we say to ourselves. A daily affirmation and mantra practice can aid in raising our vibrations and frequencies, ensuring we are being kind in our speech to ourselves and others.

Section 1 – Discipline your Senses to Purify Your Mind, Body and Soul Through Your Spiritual Practice

<u>Discipline in Silence</u>

<u>Overview</u>

Discipline in silence is the practice of turning off our senses and connection to the outside world and stimuli. We can connect to the source by turning within and silencing our "sense telephones." There are varying forms of this discipline such as silent meditation or brining oneself into a flow state through exercise or yoga. Through silent meditation we allow our hearts to open and our mind to connect and get "downloads" from the source or divine consciousness. This opens us up to insights and clarity on everyday personal and business issues we encounter. Silence is one of the most essential practices on the road to self-realization.

Self-realization is a profound spiritual state where one directly perceives and experiences their true nature beyond the body and mind. They connect to their soul and realize the divine's omnipresence. Through self-realization, one recognizes that they are spirit having a human experience, and that their spiritual soul animates their body. Upon this realization, they can release the shackles of their ego and reconvene with the divine, allowing them to realize the omnipresence and unity with divine consciousness.

The practice of this discipline allows ones to sit in silence and align with the frequency of the divine. While words are energy, silence is the source of that energy. It is through silence we become fluent in the unspoken language of truth that is divine consciousness.

We need to silence our sense telephones to disconnect from Maya. Maya is a term referenced in various spiritual faiths and is deeply connected to the importance of practicing discipline in silence. It is seen as an impediment to our spiritual growth. The literal translation is "illusion" or "magic." More specifically, it states that the illusion or delusion of the physical world which we perceive is not actually to our benefit and that each person's perception is different.

This illusion is created by the signals one takes in through our five senses, which are sight, smell, touch, sound, and taste. How we process them in the physical body and the world around us is how we interpret our environment. Some also consider the sixth sense as a collective culmination of all the other senses.

As we take in external stimuli through our senses, we create an illusion of what we perceive is happening to us, around us, and within us. However, this is an illusion created by the mindstuff, as no two people are interpreting the situation and stimuli around them in the same manner. This illusion keeps us connected to our physical or gross body and pushes us further away from Higher Frequencies such as Love and Enlightenment, or as some like to state, the Source, divine consciousness.

Through the discipline of silence, we can create stillness from the happenings around us, thus opening ourselves to direct messaging from the source. When we arrive in silence through silent meditation or flow state activities, our connection to divine consciousness becomes unobstructed. The noise of our thoughts cease, and the outside is no longer a distraction or obstacle to our journey toward enlightenment. The answers we have been searching for begin to flow as we lean into our faith and trust in the divine and feel its light and presence.

It is our goal in raising our frequencies to move from the physical body to recognition of the astral body, and ultimately to the understanding of the causal body as it connects us to the source on our journey to enlightenment.

Our Physical or Gross Body is the human body which we live in during this life. It is directly connected to the five senses. It is simply the vehicle during our physical incarnation and ultimately is perishable. It impedes our spiritual growth by keeping our soul and connection to the source rooted in the physical world and under the illusion of our senses or Maya.

Our Astral (Subtle) Body is composed of our mind and prana. Prana, also known as life force, spirit energy, or breath of life, is the energy that is associated with our higher frequencies and surrounds us in the universe. Our energy centers, chakras, transmit this energy through our nadis, or subtle energy channels. The more centered we are, and the more we align our chakras, the more we can harmoniously transmit this energy for balance in this physical life of the mind, body, and soul.

Nadis are the energy channels that connect our chakras and keep the flow of life force or prana moving in a harmonious fashion. Most of us are aware of our seven core chakras: the root for grounding and stability, the sacral for creativity and flow, the solar plexus for personal power and confidence, the heart for love and connection, the throat for communication and expression, the third eye for intuition and awareness, and the crown for higher consciousness and spiritual connection.

From our Heart Chakra, we have 108 nadis that communicate, provide energy, and transfer healing and life force to our other core six chakras. But as we dive deeper, we learn that there are 114 chakras throughout the body that are connected by 72,000 nadis. Our emotions with ourselves and others can either allow our energy to flow freely, providing life force to these chakras or our emotions can cause blocks to our energy flow which can eventually manifest in physical ailments such inflammation and disease.

When energy is blocked, we cause harm to our energy channels and chakras similar to how harm is caused by blood clots in our circulatory system. Rather than damage to our physical organs, there is damage to our life-sustaining energy centers, our chakras. Cleansing occurs through your practice of meditation and silencing the sense telephones.

Our Causal Body, as it relates divine consciousness, is the realization that the highest frequencies of the universe are omnipresent and all connected. There is no us, there is no them, as we are all one connection of energy. We are the energy, the energy is us, and we are one with the Creator, divine consciousness. Through this energy all things can manifest, and we can attain bliss and enlightenment.

As we turn within and connect to the source, we can find love, joy, happiness, and bliss resting in our heart center and connected to all things. This can only occur from turning off our sense telephones.

Another way to look at this is through the lens of Kabbalah and elevating through the four worlds. Asiyah is the physical realm. It is the animating force in the body, and where physical action occurs in tangible form. Yetzirah is the world of formation and focuses on our emotional and spiritual being. It is what defines our moral character. In this world, we focus on devotion, prayer, and our emotional relationship with the divine. Berish is the world of creation, and it is the beginning of our individualized spiritual existence. It strengthens our awareness and connection to the soul. Here, we experience deep intuitive understanding, spiritual contemplation, and intellectual awareness of God. Atzilut is The World of Emanation, a world of pure divine light and unity. This is the world of pure divine forces. This world is so close to the Divine Source that the separation ceases to exist. It is pure light and oneness. Though our discipline in silence we can move through these worlds, strengthening our connectivity to divine consciousness.

It is important to take notice of the similarities between the faiths. Both discuss similar theories but use different names. It is a reminder that we are all on the path to enlightenment, and there is no need to compare or criticize each other's paths. The roads all lead back to divine consciousness, source energy. If our paths do not preach conversion, or discount another's, and are centered in divinity and love, there should be no issues between the faiths.

Too often we fail to see the same thread of spiritualty that weaves through all the great religions and faiths. We are in a time of enlightenment; we should have a love and respect for each other's journey and faiths. Through this we can all come together in divinity as one family and bring focus to making sure we all have our physical and spiritual needs met in this incarnation.

It is my opinion that silent meditation, not prayer, is the most direct route to turn off our sense telephones. As with prayer, we still have an active mind that is interacting with our belief system and asking for help in some form or manner based on the reality we have created and our faith. Rather, with meditation we are going into deep silence, and we are opening ourselves up to receive messages from the universe, the divine, the source. We are not asking but rather receiving.

When we silence our sense telephones and reach for higher frequencies, we remove ourselves from Maya, the illusion we live under in our physical bodies. Through this silence we can align the energy or prana that exists in the Astral Body, ultimately attaining bliss through the direct connection and recognition that we are all one, we are all part of one source of energy, and all things are possible when we turn within to the heart center.

Understand that this takes practice and does not come easily or overnight. But this is our souls' journey, and we must practice discipline. We can use tools from various religious teachings, prayer, and meditation to aid us and move us closer and closer to the frequencies of bliss and enlightenment.

One of the major obstacles to practicing this discipline is the ego. It is impossible to become still if the ego is driving our behaviors and decision. The purpose of your body is to allow you to know God/the source. But to do this, one must turn inward and practice silence.

One practical guide to accomplishing this is enumerated in the eight limbs of yoga, a form of spiritual practices which can be found in the Yoga Sutras of Patanjali:

1) **The Yamas (Restraints):** Refers to restraints, moral vows, and disciplines. It encompasses an individual's interaction with the world—their disciplines, practices, and integrity—and how they conduct themselves in life. In other words, Yama teaches the attitudes to follow in the environment around us. They are:

   a) Ahimsa (nonviolence)

   b) Satya (truthfulness)

   c) Asteya (nonstealing)

   d) Brahmacharya (continence)

   e) Aparigraha (non-covetousness)

2) **The Niyamas (Observances/Disciplines):** Personal practices to purify the mind, body and soul. They deal with

self-discipline that also influences the outside world. "Ni" in Niyama means "within" in Sanskrit. They are:

a) Saucha (cleanliness)

b) Santosha (contentment)

c) Tapas (heat)

d) Svadhyaya (self-study)

c) Ishvara Pranidhana (surrendering to the divine)

3) **Asana (Postures)**: Asana means posture. You may be able to relate posture with the thought—the body is a temple. These physical poses prepare the body to be healthy, strong, and steady for meditation. While the mind is crucial, having a healthy body enables diving deeper and exploring oneself at the spiritual level.

4) **Pranayama (Breath):** What we know as breath control in English is Pranayama in Sanskrit. Controlling breath gives you power over your respiratory process and helps you understand your mind, emotions, and breath. Pranayama promotes rejuvenation, improving your physical self, and extending life.

5) **Pratyahara (Conscious Withdrawal of Senses):** In this state, our senses are devoid of engagement with the external environment. We are aware of everything around, yet we are detached from our senses. Pratyahara allows us to look at ourselves objectively, checking our habits and behaviors that negatively affect our lives and promoting betterment.

6) **Dharana (Concentration):** Dharana means attention. Here we focus our attention on a single point or object, training the mind to be steady. This calms your mind and slow down your thoughts.

7) **Dhyana (Meditation):** It is the state of uninterrupted concentration, but unlike Dharana, it is the state of being aware without focus. You can feel your mind become still. Dhyana boosts concentration, leaving little to no space for external thoughts, and helps achieve deep rest. Contemplation beyond concentration.

8) **Samadhi (Witness Consciousness):** All the above steps lead to the ultimate state of consciousness—the absorption of the self—Samadhi. In this state, your focus merges with you, and you transcend yourself, forming a connection with the divine consciousness. It is the true experience of bliss. Once a person attains the ability to see equally without distractions from the mind, it leads to the end goal—moksha (permanent freedom).

When we practice silence, we allow for the necessary space for the positive, spiritual experiences to rise to the front of our being. We allow for the positive flow of thought to guide us on our journey through the game of life. Many times in life, our overactive imagination has us focusing on the wrong things. We tend to focus on the negative things happening and not the amazing spiritual blessings that are occurring all around us. This can lead us to thinking that the world and others owe us something. Nobody owes you anything; you choose the road less traveled. It is your healing to own and your journey to enlightenment.

We must be clear here; this discipline does not always mean bringing the body and mind to a complete standstill or giving you emotional whiplash. We understand that we are all part of this world and remember the saying "you can be in it but not of it." We can move toward silence through practicing non-attachment to our emotions and material items.

When we practice non-attachment and letting go of emotions, people, places, and things that do not serve us, we open our energy up to what does. As we create space, we create silence, and through this silence we move toward witness consciousness, thus being in the world but not of it. It is through these practices that we begin to free ourselves from lower states of consciousness and open ourselves up to experiencing our higher self, thus leading to unlimited supply of bliss; bliss on tap.

We also waste lots of energy when we don't practice silence, with respect to speaking. Too often we get involved in arguments or discussions that do not raise on frequencies. We must learn to give our mouths a break so we can allow new knowledge to enter the mind. If we are constantly engaging in conversation with others and self, then we do not have time to gain new knowledge. These conversations become an energy drain and deplete us of gaining needed knowledge from the source. It is through silence that we can store, reserve, and focus our energy on life happenings that raise our vibration and bring us closer to the source.

The ultimate silence we are speaking of is that of the mind. The overall goal here is detach yourself from thinking. When we sit in a silent meditation, our minds have a moment to stop racing from thought to thought, trying to fill endless desires and passing judgment on ourselves and others. We must pause all this thinking and call in the higher frequencies around us, directly tapping into divine consciousness.

Understanding that that all things are interconnected by energy and frequency, meditating and being in silence, gives space to these energies to form clear connections without the interference of our mind. This allows for breakthroughs in all aspects of life. That is why it is important to have discipline in silence.

The Victim and Silence

Noise, noise, noise…that is all the victim hears. The noise of past pain, the noise of past defeat, the noise of suffering and the noise of trauma. When one is so attached to their past, they find it near impossible to disconnect from their senses. They cannot silence the pain and suffering of yesterday, and therefore are in a constant state of unrest. This is the victim's reality.

When they are not focused on their pain and suffering, they look to fill the void with distractions to avoid what lies beneath. They fear silence as it leaves them alone with their inner chaos. The victim looks to fill the void with distractions or noise.

Their mind is always active and runs from one negative thought to the next, never giving themselves an opportunity to make space for purification and healing. How can one practice silence if they are always preaching their pain to others and themselves? How can one ever find mental peace?

The Victim is fully immersed in Maya. This is not a place one wants to be. When you play the victim, you never give yourself a chance to grow, as the noise of life is deafening. They are a novice at best when it comes to meditation, as they are entangled in their narrative of pain.

The victim resists silence as it exposes their pain. This makes their breath irregular. They cling to the identity of the noise in their head and the noise around them. They cannot hear divinity whisper to them; they cannot connect to the source and therefore cannot heal.

The Survivor and Silence

It can feel like a constant therapy session with the survivor, both for themselves and others. They have begun to learn the art of meditation and modalities to silence their sense telephones. However, they continue to replay the past in their mind and remain attached to the story of what they needed to overcome and how hard the journey has been.

How can one truly silence their mind to gain new downloads on life if they are still constantly watching the old picture and sounds pass by? You cannot watch two movies at once. An important part of silence is having the discipline to be in the present moment without lamenting on the past or worrying about the future.

For the survivor, the past defines them, and if they truly practice discipline in silence and shut off their sense telephones, then the past ceases to exist. Their identity ceases to exist. That is the ego is its purest form, and it is why this discipline is difficult for the survivor. However, they are on the journey to enlightenment, and they make all efforts to meditate and bring themselves into varied flow states.

The survivor can use mantra repetition, binaural beats, and other frequencies to assist in silencing the mindchatter. Just as a child has training wheels on their bicycle, the survivor needs training wheels for their meditation practice. And through the use of these aides, they can practice a form of discipline in silence or meditation. But they fail to fully surrender to the flow.

Another way to look at mindchatter is the ongoing, often involuntary stream of internal dialogue that arises as your mind processes sensory input from the external world through your sense telephones. It's the voice in your head that speaks to you through judgments, fears, memories, comparisons, and other negative narratives. It impedes your journey to enlightenment. When your senses are undisciplined, they are constantly bringing in new stimuli, and your reactive mind creates mindchatter. It is ego-based, and stems from comparison, attachment, aversion, and desire. It does not serve your highest self.

While the survivor can apply silence to avoid or overcome pain, they cannot fully surrender. Their breath is strained as they are constantly analyzing their identity even during meditation. They still choose to speak over the voice of the divine even when they are tapped into this source energy and recognize it is within them.

The Warrior and Silence

The warrior doesn't need to completely shut off their sense telephones to practice discipline in silence. Yes, they can sit in meditation, turn within, connect to divine consciousness, and receive source information. But the warrior also can enter flow states, to create a silence around them and a connection to the divine while still being present and active in this world.

Silence for the warrior is not a passive act. It is way for them to practice restraint and shield against distraction, gossip, and energy leakage. Through silence, the warrior can listen to the voice within, divine consciousness, to arrive at decision with clarity and intuition.

While the warrior practices silent meditation multiple times a day, they also silence their sense telephones through physical fitness activities such as running, endurance biking, swimming, yoga, and breathwork. Through these activities, the warrior can silence the sense telephones that create mindchatter. While they are present in the activity, the world around them turns into a silent movie. They are moving through it, and at the same time, directly receiving downloads from divine consciousness.

They see silence as a sacred gateway where truth is reveled and ego dissolved. The art of silence is how the warrior nourishes their soul. It is how they break through the illusion of life and show up with empathy, love, and compassion for themselves and others. Through silence, they find self and tune into divine consciousness. It becomes their temple, a way of being.

One of the purest forms of silent meditation for the warrior is to sit in Vipassana. Vipassana, meaning "insight" or "clear seeing," is a meditative discipline rooted in silent observation, particularly of sensations, thoughts, and breath, and is usually done for multiple weeks. Silence in Vipassana is not just the absence of speech, but a sacred container for inner awareness and liberation. Vipassana reminds us that wisdom arises from deep listening. Through this silence we begin to see clearly and get the necessary downloads to continue our journey to enlightenment. The warrior sits in Vipassana to open themselves up to receive, silence the sense telephones, and have direct line of communication to divine consciousness.

The warrior merges self with source through their meditation practice and becomes one with the silence of the universe. The warrior's breath is calm, rhythmic, and tuned to divine consciousness. The warrior identity melts away as they merge into the oneness of the universe in their meditations. Through this practice, the warrior listens more than speaks and moves in alignment with divinity.

<u>My Journey into Silence</u>

My practice of this discipline started prior to me being able to walk, which I know sounds odd and is not the case for most. I was born into a spiritual family in Brooklyn, New York in the late seventies. My mother, Rose, and father, Steve, were active members of the spiritual community all their adult lives. They had not planned on having any more children, but my mother began having a recurring dream of a soul that wanted to reenter this realm to aid in the enlightenment of others. Soon, other community members began giving her similar messages. She had not shared her dream with anyone other than my father.

Rose uses Tarot cards and connectivity to communicate with other realms. And through meditation, she delivers messages to loved ones and strangers alike. She also teaches guided meditation. Steve is a healer through touch, white light, astrology, and numerology. He guides people to become better versions of themselves in his personal life, as a former New York City probation officer, and as a member of the plant medicine community. He uses astrology and numerology daily to guide friends and family to a better understanding of happenings in their lives, giving them guidance and tools to aid in their decision-making processes in both personal and business affairs.

I was born into a family whose primary purpose was to leave people and the community in a better state of being through interactions of love, light, and healing. And much of this had to do with our families' meditation practices, willingness to sit in silence, and listen to divine consciousness.

As a toddler, my mother had me sitting in meditation in the am. She would also include me in guided meditation group lessons. In my preschool years, we would take the train from Brooklyn to her Reverends' apartment on the Upper West Side to pray and meditate. I can vaguely remember going to the Ansonia Apartment Building and sitting in group meditation on Thursday nights.

Through my parents, their guidance and teachings, I was put on a path of spiritual enlightenment upon birth, or as my mom would say, before birth, when I made the choice to come back to this realm. While my tribe is Judea, we are spiritualists, and we draw from all great faiths as in their essence they all say the same thing. Love and be love. In fact, my parents met at Christmas Mass in the middle of a blizzard in Brooklyn.

My parents made sure to expose me to various faiths through-out my childhood, and for this I am grateful and blessed. They took me to meet, meditate, and study with several prominent spiritual sages.

The spiritual presence and teachings of Rabbi Gelberman have stayed with me since our encounter when I was a young boy as well. Rabbi Joseph H. Gelberman is known as a modern master of Kabbalah and a prominent figure in the study of Jewish mysticism. He was the founder of All Faiths Seminary International.

I was blessed to have met him when I was about six years old in New York City, and he had a lasting impression on my psyche and soul. He saw the light in all religions and believed we are all brothers and sisters. He gave me a sacred medallion I keep by my bed and have tattooed on my arm.

Rabbi Gelberman integrated the ancient philosophy of kabbalah with other spiritual traditions and emphasized the importance of spiritual traditions and growth. I recently watched one of his talks from 1995 which was given at a Hindu temple. His wish was that all religions met on their respective days of worship and rest to pray in each other's holy houses, as we are all family.

Another happening as a child brought me into the study of Buddhism. My parents were going to a Buddhist Temple to pray, and when I asked if I could come, they laughed and said no. Upon arriving at the Temple, my parents recognized the young child who opened the door to greet them as member of my nursery school class, and at first, they didn't think much of it.

That is, until the next morning, while my mother was cooking breakfast, I came into the kitchen, crawled on top of the counter, grabbed the incense and bell that was sitting there and muttered over and over again what sounded like "Nam Myoho Renge

Kyo." As my mother stood there in disbelief, she called my father in to ask if he had said anything to me about the night before at the Buddhist Temple. He had not and was as stunned as she was, and they stood there a bit perplexed.

This chant is the chanted by the Nichiren Buddhist. It was the chant that was used the previous night, and in doing so the monks burned incest and rang bells. My mother spoke to her spiritual guides, and they were not surprised that I had started chanting. They said I asked to go and for good reason. It seems I was a Buddhist monk in a former life; the chant was still with me. It is one of the chants I still use to this day in my a.m. and p.m. meditations.

Later in life, I began to get into the physical aspect of yoga, and soon was introduced to Autobiography of a Yogi by Paramahansa Yogananda who founded the Self-Realization Fellowship (SRF). They had many locations in California, and one of the most spectacular was Lake Shrine in the Pacific Palisades in California.

Being that I lived about twenty-five minutes away, I really wanted to go check it out. I kept setting reminders in my calendar to go, but kept pushing off the visit. One day, while I was at a market in Santa Monica, I began speaking with an Indian Businessman about Higher Frequencies and spirituality. We hit it off right away, and as he was walking away, I said we should grab a drink, even though I wasn't really drinking at the time. He turned to me without hesitation and said, "Why don't we go meditate in the gardens at Lake Shrine?"

Lake Shrine is one of the locations of the Self Realization Fellowship and where Paramahansa Yogananda spent much of his time. It is one of the few places outside of India that Ghandi's ashes are scattered. It is a highly spiritualized place where all faiths and denominations come together to pray, meditate, and connect to divine consciousness. I highly recommend making it a stop if you are ever in Los Angeles.

A few weeks later, I was mentioning that I had went there to a colleague in the cannabis business. He looked at me and said he goes on Sundays as the monks lead a guided meditation and faith talk. This all came at a time of isolation and loneliness for me and for many others immediately following the Covid lockdowns. Every Sunday thereafter I was there, and Kriya Yoga became a part of my life, meditation practices, and state of being.

I cannot help but think that the lineage of the masters of Kriya Yoga, Mahavatar Babaji, Lahiri Mahasaya, Swami Sri Yukteswar, and Paramahansa Yoganada were guiding me back to one of my many spiritual homes. While I no longer live in driving distance of Lake Shrine, I make it a point, a priority, to listen to Kriya Yoga faith talks on YouTube multiple times a week. I also incorporate the lessons into my daily meditations. Once again, when you are on the path, the path will be illuminated for you.

These sages are a few of the teachers I have been blessed to encounter in the physical and metaphysical realm on my journey to enlightenment. Whether you meet individuals like this in real time, read their teachings, or listen to recordings, their energy and spirit permeate your soul, and you are a better human for having crossed and learned from their paths.

Now, let's touch a bit on the flow state and finding silence through your physical fitness routine. I find some of my best downloads come through when I am doing yoga, running, or endurance biking. One might ask how you can be in silence, a meditative state, when doing these activities. I challenge you to think what the word silence means given our discussion above. Silence doesn't always mean there is no physical noise, or you have a lack of awareness to your surroundings. Silence doesn't necessarily mean stillness.

The goal of all spiritual practices is to return one to their breath. Your breath is your life force; your breath reconnects you to divine consciousness. Your breath relaxes your nervous system and silences the chatter of your mind. Through the silence of your mindchatter, your become more connected to the energy that guides you.

Through practices like yoga, running, and biking, you also must have extreme focus. In yoga, this is referred to as Drishti, which is when you focus your gaze on a point so you can enhance your concentration and mindfulness. It is a way to silence the outside world and turn within.

At first, this may seem like an opposing thought process, practicing discipline in silence through physical fitness, but I and others can attest that some of our most poignant downloads come when we silence the outside world through these activities and only can hear the voice from within. Looking at physical fitness in this manner brings a new appreciation to the experience, as it has as much to do with your mental health as your physical health.

My goal in sharing these stories with you is not for you to try to follow suit, but rather an example of how my journey in the discipline has evolved and continues to evolve over time. As should yours. You should be open to learning new techniques. But do not jump from one technique to the next, as this will get you nowhere fast. And I don't subscribe that if you aren't having success with the one started that you should jump to the next. If a modality was calling you to try it in the first place, you will find the success you need with it eventually.

In my experience, silencing the mindchatter is all about habits and routine, specifically as it relates to your personal spiritual practice and personal physical fitness routine. I am repetitively using the word personal for a reason here; there is no magic bullet when it comes to this. You need to try various modalities and see which ones work for you. They need to both fit in your schedule and give yourself the silence and space to connect you to your inner voice, divine consciousness.

You also must realize that you are a work in progress, especially when it comes to meditation. I have heard stories of many great sages and the commonality in all of them when discussing meditation is the fact that they too get distracted; they too questioned time and time again whether the mindstuff would ever shut off. But they continued in their practice, day in and day out.

I find it best to meditate first thing when I wake up, as this is when our mind is least distracted from the noise of the outside world. I also like to meditate immediately prior to sleeping so I may purify my mind of the day's noise prior to resting. I find moments when necessary, during the day, no matter the set or setting, when I feel the noise of the world weighing on me, and this is when I turn to my meditation and discipline in silence.

I make use of various techniques from various spiritualities and faiths. I find my silence through these meditation practices. Meditation practices from Judaism, Buddhism, Hinduism, Kriya Yoga, and other spiritual faiths I encounter on my journey. There are so many wonderful practices across various spiritualities and faiths.

Breakthroughs and downloads from source happen in the moments in between. The moments in between the noise, the moments where the world goes silent, and through a disciplined routine. These moments can be called into presence more often, when needed and on a more regular basis when you practice with discipline. And that is where clarity is gained and a plan can be laid out to integrate healing back into your conscious day.

When you begin a spiritual path, no matter at what point in your life, you need to be aware of the clues the energies are leaving for you on your journey. You see when you are on the spiritual path, the energies will guide you to modalities necessary for your practice. The question is, are you listening?

Your spiritual practice and your physical fitness routine serve as tools to purify your mind. They allow you to disconnect from the outside world in various manners, silencing the mindchatter that obstructs our spiritual growth.

When we find silence, we can tap into higher frequencies and arrive back at the noise of life with new clarity and momentum. May the modalities that find you and resonate with you guide you to your silence.

Discipline in Thinking and Contemplation

Overview

Our goal on the path to spiritual enlightenment, and as we move toward higher frequencies, is to come closer to attaining Witness Consciousness and realizing we are divine consciousness. Witness Consciousness is being an observer to the world as it manifests around you. Practicing non-attachment is key in this aspect of your journey; however, we need to be active participants with our environment and life. We can practice moving toward the concept of witness consciousness through discipline in thinking and contemplation.

Thinking is how we process thought through analyzation, comparison, solving problems, and planning. Our sense telephones take in stimuli and our mind, often through our ego, responds with thought. This is an active process, fast-paced, and generally goal-oriented. While thought can be logical and imaginative, without discipline it can be distracted and repetitive. We can end of up in a loop of low frequencies, and our thoughts can be shadowed by fear, shame, and anxiety.

Contemplation is more intentional and is inwardly focused. Where thinking is reactionary to the sense telephones taking in stimuli, contemplation is a pause, a pause before a pivot. A moment to reassess what was taken in and how it should be viewed. Think of contemplation as a proofread of your reality.

Contemplation removes us from the stimuli and bombardment of our personal, business and professional affairs, allowing the days information overload to settle into digestible data points. It allows you to rest and absorb the situation and look for the truth as it fits your current narrative. To pose the question to yourself, do you feel your immediate reaction was just, and what is the best way to proceed emotionally and mentally? Through silence, stillness, and openness, one can focus spiritually and philosophically on the content of the thought, giving us the necessary pause in our hectic lifestyles and allowing the energy that surrounds us to guides us into the pivots that are necessary for change.

Ultimately, we are the drivers of our reality. This is based on how our mind interprets things happening to us and around us. It is based on how we consume through our five senses and interpret with our sixth sense, the mind. Our mind is our constant companion on our spiritual journey, and it has a direct effect on how we live our lives.

In yoga studies, the mind is broken into four parts. It is helpful to look at how the mind functions and mindchatter through each of these parts. Buddhi, which is focused on the intellect, uses memories, the brain, to come to conclusions on what is happening around us and too us in real time. Intelligence, therefore, is not just book smarts; it also comes from life experiences and reasoning. As they say, some things cannot be taught in a classroom, but they are still intellectual by nature. Discipline is important here as not all decisions should be based on solely on intellect; in some cases, doing the right thing may be contrary to what our intellectual brain is thinking.

Manas is the memory that is stored in every cell of the body, not just the brain. It is also said that these memories can be generational. Generational trauma, trauma not directly experienced by you but rather through your lineage, influences this part of the mind. This is an important point, as sometimes our body is reacting on muscle memory that no longer serves us or our mental well-being. We must have an awareness and must discipline our thoughts to prevent such actions from occurring. It can be helpful to find a modality of healing, such as holotropic breathwork, yoga, or ancestral medicine that can help you work through any traumas of this incarnation as well as generational trauma.

Ahankara is the intellect that gives us a sense of identity, and it is also sometimes correlated to EGO. We want to discipline our thinking so we are not coming from a place of ego that harms our interactions with ourselves and others. It is important to have a sense of identity and define who you are to yourself and others, but it should be done with a humble demeanor. Intellect driven by Ahankara can delude our humbleness and allow our ego to lead the way. This is something we would like to avoid.

Chitti is the cosmic intelligence. It is when we can connect to the source, the divine, to garner information that is not rooted in our memory or intellect. Through meditation and forms of prayer, we can connect to this cosmic intelligence, drawing information directly from the universe. When we receive these downloads, we must integrate them into our daily lives to derive the spiritual benefits and healing. One might say Chitti is the highest achievement in the practice of disciplining one's mind.

The mind is of utmost importance when one is on their spiritual path. When we can discipline our senses to purify our mind through thinking and contemplation, we can put more focus on things such as the moving toward enlightenment and divine consciousness.

An individual can apply the concepts of faith and trust to this discipline; we will learn more about these concepts later. These concepts remind us to have faith in divine consciousness and trust that everything it brings into our life, to stop focusing, thinking, and contemplating on negativity, regret, or other stories that garner emotions that do not serve our spiritual journey. We should bring our focus to samadhi, or equanimity, the balanced state of mind in which highest level of consciousness is realized. Through this process, one can dissolve their fear and anxiety from experiences on their journey to enlightenment.

One must use contemplation in order examine their life and make the necessary changes on their path to self-realization and divine consciousness. A true seeker takes in all the information from their life experiences and uses it to improve their present state of being through contemplation. They look to see how things apply to them, their journey, and the necessary course correction that must be made along their journey. Through contemplation, one can adjust their thought process to better align with higher frequencies to purify their mind, body, and soul.

We must also practice discipline in thinking when it comes to desires. I want to be clear here that desires are not always a negative thing. I am referring here to allowing our thoughts to chase desires that can cause pain and suffering or desires that are not aligned with our highest potential. Desires can have a functional use when it comes to filling the actual needs of our body or our social contracts with others, and in these instances, they are necessary for us to survive and thrive. Chasing desires at the expense of our mental and physical well-being is ego-based and should be avoided.

What we feed our mind will also affect how we think about certain people, places, things, and situations. When we feed our mind with negative thoughts and emotions, then we will color our reaction with them. We must practice discipline in thinking and contemplation as we receive and interpret emotions and energy in our immediate environment. Otherwise, your attitude or thought process can create obstacles in your life that are unnecessary, self-created, and imaginary. To purify your mind, body, and soul, you must actively guard your thoughts. Good thoughts arise from doing the work and being an active participant in your journey toward enlightenment.

A good exercise to practice discipline in thinking is to journal your positive thoughts each day. Some may call this a practice of gratitude journaling. Then, reflect on these positive thoughts as they will take up the space and purify your mind, keeping negative thoughts to a minimum, thus allowing the mind to strengthen over time and removing any negative and useless thought process. There are no short-cuts. You must do the work, as manifestation is nothing without action, and the start of this is practicing discipline.

Your mind can either be a tool for self-realization and liberation, or it can trap you in the illusion of this world. If you do not practice discipline, the mind will follow the senses and become subservient to desire and restlessness. You must remember that thoughts carry vibrations, and these frequencies have a direct impact on the energy you attract.

This can be managed and disciplined through meditation, prayer, breathwork, and other activities that bring you into a flow state. Prayer is a bit more aligned with discipline in thinking, as it is an active process of asking divine consciousness for assistance in problem solving, whereas meditation is more helpful with contemplation, as it allows one to turn within and seek guidance from within on the obstacle or problem that is being encountered. In both cases, divine consciousness is the giver of the knowledge; in one scenario it is external and the other it is internal. It is all oneness and divinity.

Through a disciplined mind, we find freedom from pain and suffering and have compassion and empathy for ourselves and others. We find clarity in life's most difficult moments. Your thoughts, much like your speech, communicate with divine consciousness and has spiritual benefits or spiritual consequences. Your mind can and will manifest your reality.

The Victim and Thinking and Contemplation

Consumed by the negative overtones of life, the victim allows their senses to communicate feelings of fear, anxiety, pain, and suffering to the mind. The victim is not in control of their thoughts, but rather their thoughts are in control of them. Their overactive mind and negative outlook on life keeps them paralyzed from moving forward in the direction of progress.

Their actions are reactive and fear-based, and strips them of their power. The victim allows their thoughts to control their emotions and interactions with self and others, as they choose to identify with their pain. One might say they are unconscious to life, and when they contemplate, they get caught in feedback loops of trauma, blame, and helplessness.

Through their contemplation, they envision all the negative scenarios that could occur should they act, and begin to tackle the obstacles in front of them. They only see darkness and fail to recognize that through the darkness there is light, through the pain there is healing, and through the fire there are blessings.

The Survivor and Thinking and Contemplation

While the Survivor realizes that they have made it through hard times and can do it again, they sometimes get stuck in old thought patterns, allowing their mind to bring up feelings of doubt, which impairs their clarity on their past achievements. They know better, but sometimes they feel they just can't move on. They feel lethargic and tired as they are letting their thoughts turn into their own worst enemies.

The survivor can observe their thoughts, but they still have a tough time controlling them. This is due in part to the fact that the survivor holds on to old wounds and seeks external validation. They might have self-awareness, but it oscillates between doubt and empowerment.

The survivor can overcome their negative thoughts through habits and behaviors they have acquired along the journey toward enlightenment, but this is real work and integration, as they have failed to synthesize these habits and behaviors into reflexes. They must make a conscious effort to not succumb to the mindchatter during their contemplative states, as it impedes their journey and growth.

The Warrior and Thinking and Contemplation

The warrior's mind rests in equanimity. It is neither disturbed nor excited by the information that is received through their senses. Rather, they analyze the information from the seat of the witness and through a disciplined mind, eventually coming to a rational conclusion to the situation and the next steps.

Through a disciplined thought process, they understand that they will make the best decision in a calm state of mind with the facts they currently have access to at a given moment in time. To allow the mind to lament on the past or worry about the future reminds them that they are not living in the present. By controlling their mind, they find their flow state and do not allow negative thoughts to cloud their judgment or impede their progress.

The life and thought process of the warrior is one of discipline. They observe their environment and breathe through any moments of difficult. Through contemplation they turn apparent failures into lessons that allow them to elevate their way of being and consciousness. Even a curse is a blessing to the warrior as they contemplate and revel the gem or lesson hidden in the experience. They search for and arrive at truth, love, and clarity on their journey toward in enlightenment through a disciplined mind.

My Journey to Discipline My Thoughts and Contemplation

My mind has always been my worst enemy. Throughout my early life, as with many, my traumas played an active role in the negative dialogue in my head. As an overachiever, I was hypercritical in my performance. It didn't matter if it was personal, business, or scholastic; I never felt like I performed to the level I had the ability to. For some reason, my thought processes liked to play out negative scenarios. When I took time to contemplate, I found myself viewing things from a place of lack rather than abundance, and from darkness rather than light.

As an adolescent, the combination of music and physical activity such as biking or going to the gym had a profound effect on slowing my thoughts down and allowing me to process the day. Music was always a central theme in our household; whether it was going to a concert, buying album/tapes/CDs regularly (depending on the decade), or just dancing in the living room, music always helped me elevate and heal. Unfortunately, I had not learned discipline in listening yet, and some of the music I listened to at the time had negative lyrics. Lyrics are mantras, and negative lyrics carry low frequencies. We will get into this more a bit later.

I started to build my routine to get better control of my mindstuff, making sure that no matter what was going on in life, that I made time to meditate and workout. Through these activities, I was able to have better control over my thoughts and process life with a bit more ease.

However, when I wasn't doing these things, I was either working to exhaustion or out eating and drinking. While the drinking helped me calm down, it only made my thoughts more problematic the next day. At this point in my life I was still an alcohol executive, and I had just moved to back to Miami from Las Vegas. Here is a bit more color to illustrate the dilemma.

In 2015, while living in Las Vegas, an opportunity presented itself for me take an equity partnership position in a start-up champagne company. I decided this would be a good foray back into the entrepreneurial world, so I signed the contract and moved back to Miami where I would be based. The goals were to align the brand with a new importer, restrengthen its relationship with its distributor and retailers, and create a strong market segmentation/implementation strategy, eventually, preparing the brand for acquisition by a conglomerate in the space, a venture capital firm, a capital partner, or signing a celebrity that could accelerate growth.

I got to travel across the country and meet with business partners and owners from all walks of life. One day, I would be out on the street trying to sign on account in New York or Las Vegas, and then the next day I would be having a meeting with David Bonderman, the founder of TPG Capital. It soon became apparent that what the founder had told me was not the case, though, when it came to the financial health of the company.

At the same time, my eyes turned to the new green rush, cannabis. I was able to secure some funds and made an investment in a vertically operated grow in Denver, Colorado. I worked, into my already busy schedule, trips to Colorado to learn the business of cannabis. I believed a similar brand development and distribution strategy to alcohol could be applied to the cannabis market. All during this time, problems were continually mounting in the champagne business and in my mind. My thinking was undisciplined, and I was having issue cutting through the noise to contemplate my next steps.

And then she began calling: Mother Ayahuasca. While I had taken my fair share of mind-altering substances, I hadn't yet heard of her. But the more I learned, the more intrigued I became with wanting to sit in ceremony. Friends of mine had suggested I sit with their medicine worker in California, which I was scheduled to do. But fate intervened, and I pivoted to have a meeting with Sammy Hagar (Van Halen) and Bob Weir (Grateful Dead) to discuss launching a cannabis company. Although there were no mind-altering substances, the conversation was interplanetary.

I couldn't shake the call of Mother Ayahuasca, and through my network, it was suggested that I go to SpiritQuest in Peru. It was the summer of 2016 that I began this phase of my healing. This is one of the original medicine retreats which was run by a gringo, Don Howard, who has since passed. The ceremonies were officiated by 3rd and 4th generation Chavin Shamans of the Shipibo tribe. It is nestled outside of Iquitos on the Rio Napa River about fifteen minutes from where the Rio Napa and Amazon meet. We gathered on sacred land, home to the Shipibo tribe, the holders of this medicine. This experience would forever change the course of my life.

It took over twenty-four hours of planes, taxis, buses, and river boats to arrive at SpiritQuest, and I would not be leaving for the next eight nights and nine days. I would sit with a group of almost thirty people in four ceremonies during my stay. Through these ceremonies, I began the healing process of my mind, body, and spirit. It was the beginning of a longer journey to heal various traumas and years of self-inflicted physical and mental abuse.

Healing is a journey, not a destination. I want to be clear; Ayahuasca is not a cure. Ancestral medicine reconnects you to breath, your ancestors, and divine consciousness. There are moments in ceremony where you look down on your avatar and no longer are aligned with what you see, but it is up to you to do the work. A restructuring of mind, body, and soul through a disciplined practice rooted in contemplation and changing one's way of thinking.

After ceremony, the work begins, through journaling, shadow work, integration, and forming new habits through discipline; you become a better version of yourself. But many do not do the work that it takes following ceremony. The work is a dissociation from people, places, habits, and behaviors that no longer serve you on your journey to enlightenment. The work can be isolating and lonely, but the work aligns you with higher frequencies.

Integration takes time, patience, and persistence. Too many people are looking for a quick fix and run back to the medicine too often; they do not trust in the process. They receive the downloads, but fail to ever integrate the messages and heal. We will get into this more later in the book.

Following the ceremonies, it was clear to me I needed to exit the alcohol space. The alcohol space provided a great education for the next phase of my mission, but it was no longer in alignment with what I came back to this incarnation to accomplish. The overall message was clear; I was to build brands that were vehicles for change and healing.

In our society, brands are demi-gods. We need to infuse them with spirituality and well-being, teachings that raise our vibration and the collective vibration of society. We need to infuse them with messages of higher frequencies and modalities of healing. The brands are the trojan horses to return the masses to spirituality and whole-life wellness. I pivoted once again with a focus on the cannabis space and my continued spiritual, physical, and mental well-being journey.

My work with ayahuasca began my process to learn to let go of limiting beliefs and the traumas that caused them. It began the process of me learning to take control of my mind and have the discipline over it; to be less negative and less reactionary.

Over the next eight years, I continued to work with this medicine and others, allowing me to integrate new habits and behaviors in my life that had a profound effect on taking control of my thoughts and mind. I became a certified yoga teacher, which launched me into the study of ancient yogic philosophies. I found Kriya yoga, the path to Self-Realization, and began visiting Lake Shrine in Los Angeles for prayer and meditation. I greatly benefited from my visits and the weekly faith talks given by the monastic, and I rediscovered my Judaism and began mystic Judaic Studies, all of which have been incorporated to into my daily habits to assist in the discipline of my thoughts and contemplation.

I also found my nutritional and psychical fitness regimens taking on new life. Endurance biking, running, and shopping at the farmers market all became the norm. One might ask how this relates to discipline in thinking and contemplation. One word: BREATH. All these activities returned me to my breath; they taught me how to breathe through the dissonance and noise. And once you can breathe through the dissonance, your mind can become calm, clear, and disciplined.

I now have the modalities to calm my mind and return me to my breath. My discipline in thinking and contemplation is accomplished and aided by my spiritual practice, my physical fitness routine, and my nutritional behavior. Through these habits and behaviors, I have learned to calm my mind when my thoughts are racing, and things seem out of control. I pause and return to my breathe and I realize that I am all the medicine I need.

And remember sometimes…you need to give yourself grace to fall out of your discipline, realign, recalibrate and fall back in….

Section 2 – Discipline your Senses to Purify Your Mind, Body and Soul Through Your Nutritional Behavior

<u>Overview</u>

As the saying goes, you are what you eat. The food you eat can either be your medicine or your poison. It can either elevate your physical and mental health, or lead to disease, pain, and suffering. Having discipline in your nutritional behavior, your diet, is not just with respect to the types of food we put in our bodies, but it also relates to the how much and how often we eat, the origin of the food, and how the food might have been transported and processed.

The food we eat is meant to bring us closer to source energy. After eating, one should be able to achieve a deep meditative state and feel unblocked emotionally, mentally, and physically. From a young age we are focused on taste; however, the true test of food is how it makes you feel. That doesn't mean that it should taste bad. However, how the food, fuel, you take in makes you feel emotionally, physically, and mentally should take precedence over taste.

One should also ensure that their food is providing them with the correct nutrients needed for their lifestyle and body type and that they are not practicing over nutrition. Over nutrition can lead to all sorts of physical ailments. Aside from weight gain, and it can tax the body in ways that cause disease and ailments.

While processed food and refined sugars might taste good, they can wreak havoc on you physically and emotionally. Rather, when you have sugar cravings, you can turn to living foods like fruits, maple syrup, or honey. Living foods are natural foods, as close to their original pure form as possible. They are best experienced when they can be traced to their source ingredients, and preferably when those source ingredients are in season. This means there has been no chemical process to procure any ingredients that are used in your meal. This can ensure they retain all their active ingredients and nutrients. Categories of living foods are fruits and vegetables, sprouted nuts and seeds, fish, poultry, and whole grains.

It is also a good idea to try to eat regionally, ensuring that the food hasn't traveled long distances where damage could have been done to its energy. Eating regionally is most beneficial for you and the planet as well. It leaves a smaller carbon footprint as less gas was used in the food's transportation. It may also have less impurities, as there is less contact with supply chain items such as packaging, shipping vessels, and chemicals along the food's journey to your plate. Eating within your ecosystem ensures that unnecessary energy didn't encounter the food, and that the food wasn't processed. Our bodies are in tune with our environment; there is an energetic danger to eating foods that cannot grow where we are currently living.

One needs to learn to control their desires associated with their taste buds. Too often, our eating behavior is led by sensation and impulse, which has us making poor decisions. Our eating decisions are often based on the desire to keep our stomach full and our mouth happy rather than to provide our body with the nutrients it needs to fuel its activity and repair. Improper food choices and overeating can lead to fear, anxiety, and depression, as the heart, mind, and body must go into overdrive to process the food.

Food should be energy enhancing; however, if we eat too much or the wrong things, it can lead to energy depletion. This can affect us both spiritually and physically. The energy used to process food that you shouldn't have eaten is being taken away from meditation, wellness, and other life enhancing activities, leading to a misuse of our life force/prana, and laziness.

Prāṇa, or life force, is a yogic term that refers to the energy of divine consciousness that moves through us. In Kabbalistic terms, it is referred to as Ruach. I am highlighting the two different names here to draw us all back to the understanding that we are divine consciousness, no matter what faith you follow. We are all one in the same.

Our lifeforce is the subtle energy that animates all living things—it is the breath within the breath, the vibrational current that fuels our physical, mental, and spiritual vitality. Prāṇa allows us to rise into elevated states of awareness, clarity, and inner strength. It raises our vibration and brings us to higher frequencies, aiding us on our journey to enlightenment.

When we practice discipline with our nutritional behavior, eating becomes a sacred act of honoring this life force. To do so, we must choose foods rich in prāṇa. Foods rich in prana are fresh, natural, and energetically alive. We must eat with presence and intention; through this process, we strengthen our inner frequency. If we follow these guidelines, eating becomes not just nourishment, but alignment of higher frequencies.

Overeating, emotional eating, or consuming lifeless food dulls the flow of prāṇa and lowers our vibration. Some characteristics of lifeless foods are foods that are ultra-processed, have non-living ingredients with names that you cannot pronounce, and have overbearing flavor profiles that are sweet, sour, bitter, salty, astringent, and pungent.

I want to pause to discuss the word diet. The origin of the word diet comes from the Greek word diaita (δίαιτα), which originally meant "way of life" or "manner of living." One might interpret this to mean how we live a holistic lifestyle which might include food, exercise, rest, and moral discipline. Diet is a way of life and returns us to our breath. It allows one to maintain their physical and spiritual well-being. Diet was never meant to be a temporary solve; it was meant to be a way of being.

As weight issues became prevalent, savvy marketers began to use the word as technique to convince consumers that if they followed this regimen for a certain amount of time, they would reach their ideal weight. This is a losing proposition and the wrong way to look at diet. We are a culture of quick fixes, so I do not expect the "diet industry" to stop marketing quick fixes and start using the word diet correctly.

The original meaning of diet is more in alignment with how ancient faiths and the yogic lineage views nutritional behavior. Many of the great faiths speak of this in scripture. They don't mention weight, but rather food and its connectivity to the divine and the necessary rituals around that connection. Diet is a spiritual practice, not just a physical regimen. It is about discipline, spirituality, balance, and harmony with nature and self. It is the balance of emotional, physical, and mental well-being through the nutrients we consume and how we consume them.

The individual must make a choice to want to live a healthier life, the individual that is reading this book, to take control of the word diet once again and understand their nutritional behavior is way of being. What you eat, why you eat it, and what your relationship is with food should be the questions you ask when deciding what you feed your body and spirit. Start here rather than a "fad diet" that is a temporary solve. I speak from experience, having had weight issues most of my life and tried them all. It wasn't until I looked at the word diet as a lifestyle and examined my relationship with food that I arrived at my ideal weight. But more on this in a bit.

We can affirm our devotion to living from a higher place when we practice mindful and intentional eating. It is at these points that each choice, each bite, becomes an act of self-respect and spiritual alignment. Too often, eating becomes an action. It lacks awareness.

We should have an awareness that allows us to practice restraint and reverence, allowing the body to flourish from the fuel we serve it. I consider eating to be a form of meditation, and therefore your mind is a product of the food you eat. When we eat with awareness, we can avoid unnecessary disease and sufferings and limit our exposure to needing doctors and medicine. This allows us to have more peaceful life.

For most of us, we live in abundance. And this is true with our eating behavior as well. We turn to food for enjoyment, not fuel. We eat when we are anxious, and we eat our trauma as we find comfort in the addictive foods that are readily available. You are supposed to eat when you are hungry, not for the sake of emotional fulfillment. Overeating is essentially trying to over fill a gas tank for car, except your body stores the excess as fat and negative energy. It doesn't have the means or capacity to burn it off. And what did you get out of it? A moment of chemical elations, a dopamine hit, that leaves physical and emotional scars.

Our food is used to purify our mind and body. When we purify our mind and body, we become unshakable by life. This allows us to arrive at perceived problems with equanimity and an open heart, thus aiding in our journey to enlightenment and attunement/attainment of higher frequencies.

Discipline in our nutritional behavior is not so much about how we physically look. This is something the media, the medical industry, and fad diets would have you believe. Rather, this discipline is focused on what fuel we feed our body and mind and how it connects us or disconnects to divine consciousness. We are more in tune with our higher self the greater discipline in our nutritional behavior we practice. When you eat, you need to ask yourself: is this good fuel for my mind, body, or soul? Is the food I am about to eat polluting me or purifying me?

The Victim and Nutritional Behavior

There are many types of eating disorders, but one common thread in almost all of them is eating from emotional entanglement or trauma. This is clearly a victim mentality. Food becomes a way to escape emotional pain such as shame, anxiety, fear, or loneliness. It is when one turns to food to numb, escape, or compensate for unmet emotional and spiritual needs. Nutritional behavior from the victim mindset is reactive, not intentional, in nature and harmful to the physical and spiritual bodies.

We must remember that food carries vibration. And when someone is vibrating at a low frequency, they may feel heavy, dull, and lethargic. Anyone who has felt this way, possibly due to being hungover or depressed, knows that they crave unhealthy, dense, processed foods. This is when we make the poorest decisions in our eating behavior. We have all been there at one time or another, but some are stuck in this behavior, specifically those with a victim mentality.

These types of foods that are impure and overstimulating can also weaken our ability to connect to the divinity through meditation. This eating behavior hinders our ability to purify our mind and body and tune into higher frequencies.

Just think of how you feel after you eat junk food or fast food. Do you want to meditate after? Do you want to work out? Are you depressed and lethargic? If something makes you feel this way, why would you continue to reinjure yourself by eating it? It may be because you are stuck in a victim mentality and are doing it unconsciously to sooth your emotional pain with the wrong medicine.

When it comes to their eating behavior, those who have the mentality of a victim may tend to have a shallower, heavier breath. As you become more disciplined in your eating, and you begin to view food as part of your journey to enlightenment, your breath becomes lighter as well.

The victim eats to feel something. But as mentioned above we eat for fuel to feed our life force. When we eat to feel something, we disregard the primary reason we eat, and we look toward momentary gratification rather than long term health, sustenance, and physical and mental well-being.

The Survivor and Nutritional Behavior

As we move onto the survivor, their eating habits have partial awareness. They have begun to connect their eating behavior with health, healing, and possibly discipline. However, they find themselves still attached to their trauma, and in doing so, tend to waiver from a restricted nutritional lifestyle to pure indulgence to sooth their unresolved issues. The survivor also likes to boast and use their nutritional behavior as a form of superiority or identity.

The survivor may look to foods that are energizing and healthy but still turn to foods that are poor in nutritional value when they are stressed or emotionally overstimulated. They are beginning to see food as more than nourishment. They understand food is a spiritual act and has a direct impact on our frequencies. Often, food is fuel to the survivor.

The Warrior and Nutritional Behavior

The warrior practices discipline in their nutritional behavior as they view food as part of their spiritual journey and a key component to their spiritual enlightenment. Their nutritional behavior is viewed as a sacred communion, an opportunity to give thanks for the nourishment of living food that connects us to the air we breathe, the land we live on, and ultimately divine consciousness.

The warrior finds their nourishment in foods that are pure, energetically clean, and that have been minimally processed or not processed at all. And if the foods are processed, it is in a manner that combines living foods but does not distort the source ingredients or their nutritional value. They listen to the body, eating by intuition rather than by cravings and emotions.

It is important to for the warrior to bless their food before consumption, as each bite signifies their faith in higher frequencies and divine consciousness. The warrior tastes the essence of life, of divinity, in each bite and gives thanks for its availability, access, and nourishment. They don't eat to satisfy their ego but rather to elevate the sparks of holiness.

My Journey to Discipline My Nutritional Behavior

So how does one put all this into practice? There is a great deal of high-level thinking above, but we must live in the real world. We have hectic daily lives and live in urban metropolises where temptation is everywhere. Food companies hide behind laws to create labels that use words that promote health. However, behind the wrapper is something that is filled with unhealthy, ultra processed ingredients and has a highly addictive nature. I am not just talking about the junk food market; this also goes for the "health" foods market.

While I am not a dietician, doctor, or nutritionist; this is an area where I can speak from personal experience. Most of my life, I struggled with my weight. I always say I had a choice growing up in NYC and going to NYC public school: be the fat kid who was picked on or be the tough guy. I choose the tough guy, as it was easier to mask my insecurities with aggression and wordplay than allow others to be abusive to me.

By the time I was thirteen, I was already 240 lbs and 5'10". As an adolescent, I tried weight watchers, Nutrisystem, and a host of other "diets." I went to weight loss camp as a teenager where they put us on limited calorie diets. At points, I was able to lose the weight, but it always seemed to find me.

Throughout my adolescent teenage years and early adult life, I struggled with my weight. I was fortunate that I carried it well and I worked out, but I was still overweight. I made every excuse possible as to why I couldn't keep the weight off. I constantly played the victim. You see, many people in my family had weight problems. The easiest scapegoat was genetics, and that was partly true, as many people in my lineage coped with personal and generational trauma through overindulgence with food, eating the wrong things, and overeating.

Part of the problem was not taking responsibility for my own actions. I had no discipline when it came to my nutritional behavior. Food was a coping mechanism for personal and generational trauma; I found comfort in eating. While my physical fitness routine was taking shape, it is said your nutritional behavior is 80 percent of the battle, and it was a battle I was constantly losing. I mean, it's just a treat, right? Well, a treat is something that occurs once in a while, not daily or hourly.

There has always been an overabundance of fad diets, pills, and potions. The problem is that these quick fixes temporally get the weight off but don't instill the necessary new habits to keep the weight off. They don't allow you to deal with the trauma that might be causing you to overeat, nor do they give you the practical tools to make the correct choices when eating.

My view of diet and my eating behavior changed in 2010. While I was living in Las Vegas, I ballooned up to 280lbs, and was not comfortable in my own skin. At the time, I was an executive in Vegas and had the keys to the castle when it came to overindulgence with expensive food and liquor. My buddy Bill, who was an executive in the travel sector, asked me to come meet him in Mexico with his trainer David. David is a health and fitness couch for NBA Players and hotels around the world. Bill simply said, "You're better than the way you are treating yourself," which no one ever said to me before.

Generally, when people tell you that you need to lose weight, it is in a derogatory and shameful manner. The delivery of the message was with love and kindness. They removed the short-term concept of diet from my mindstuff and replaced it with lifestyle changes, ones that I could incorporate into my daily behavior. Bill also took me grocery shopping and showed me how many healthy food labels were misleading. This was my first foray into learning how to read a label.

We also worked on my physical fitness routine. I always was of the thought process that so long as my chest was bigger than my belly, and I did cardio and weightlifted, I was good to go. They introduced me to high-intensity interval training (HIIT) and gave me a regimen that insured I was burning fat and building muscle, the aspects of a proper physical fitness routine. This is something you need to explore with a professional. There are plenty of apps now that use AI to assist in configuring a program to your body type. We will get into this more in the chapter on physical fitness.

This helped for the next few years, but my lifestyle didn't change. I still seesawed between 220 and 240. I had not dealt with the reason I was an overeater or why I turned to food and alcohol to cope with life. I was still blaming the externalities of life and others for my fluctuation in weight; this is a victim mentality. For example, while in the alcohol industry, I had to entertain people at dinners and nightclubs. Each time I would put a few pounds back, I would blame my current lifestyle but wouldn't take responsibility for lacking discipline and self-control in these settings. While I no longer identified as the fat kid, I still had a weight issue. I was surviving, but I wasn't thriving. I know now the reason was I still was trying to treat the symptom, which was my weight, and not the cause, which was my trauma and how it affects my mindstuff.

My healing of my trauma began with my work with Mother Ayahuasca. This truly began the first phase of healing in a way I never thought possible. My physical purge was one of mind, body, and soul. I felt energies that no longer serving me exited me. My skin purged liquid and odors that reminded me of those on the ground after Mardi Gras in New Orleans, years of overindulgence with alcohol and food. I was now on my journey to healing and finding my nutritional behavior.

What I did not know was that along the journey I had to burn my former self to the ground, including my nutritional behavior and physical fitness routine, which were a major part of the integration to follow. Part of this integration was to rid myself of the trauma around food and practice discipline in my nutritional behavior. Up to now, I had coped with my generational and personal trauma through food and my eating habits, through overeating and making poor nutritional choices.

Through my medicine work and my spiritual and religious studies, I soon realized that there was no one to blame but myself. I could deflect all I want, but I needed to have discipline of my senses and really work through my nutritional behavior. I needed to recognize the fact that I turned to food to sooth my anxiety, as many overeaters do. Lastly, I needed to get the idea of short-term diet out of my head and look to long-term habits.

Over the next few years, I had a new outlook on my health. I no longer viewed the word diet as temporary solve, but rather as a lifestyle. My relationship with alcohol also changed. I still enjoyed a drink, but I didn't consume like I used to. The less I drank, the more I saw that when I did, it had a clear detrimental effect on my physical, mental, and emotional health.

Over the next few years, my weight began to stabilize between 210 and 220, which was still not great, but better than I had been in the past. Integration after a spiritual experience can take a few years. One must remember that it takes ninety days to turn a new behavior into a habit. In my experience, when you try to change many behaviors at once, you end up failing at them all.

You see, a diet is a way of life. It refers to a sustainable, holistic approach to eating and living that supports long-term health, vitality, and balance—physically, mentally, and spiritually. These short-term "diet programs" focused on restriction, weight loss, or rigid rules. They were temporary solves that set you up for long term failure.

I carried on the lessons of reading labels of food but took it one step further. I began going to farmers markets and sourcing living foods that were within my geography. While I indulged in certain things from time to time, I predominately shopped at these markets. Ultra processed foods lost their appeal, as they made my mind and body lethargic.

The second phase began during the lockdowns of Covid. I feel blessed to have experienced lockdown in the manner I did, looking into the mirror of myself, asking the hard questions, and making the necessary changes. Fortunately, the farmers markets remained open for the most part. The new variable was that restaurants were closed and so was take out, allowing me to further heal and explore my relationship with food. I began to experiment with my cooking, making healthy and mindful choices.

My feeling during Covid was that we were in a health war, and I was going to double down on my wellness choices, especially with the food/fuel I put in my body. It was a simple choice we all had; you could evolve or devolve, but there was no in-between.

My discipline in eating became stronger, and my new nutritional behaviors became habits. And being that the gyms were closed and I had all this new energy from mindful and disciplined eating, I began running, endurance biking, and did my 200-hour yoga certification virtually. Had I not found discipline in my nutritional behavior, none of this would have been accomplishable.

I also made a consciousness choice to not get on the scale. I felt this trapped me in the mindset of the short-term diet and not the ethos of the word diet according to a way of being. When I finally went for my first physical after lockdown and got on the scale, it read 182. Over the last few years, my weight has stayed between 176 and 185. I no longer beat myself up when I fall out of my discipline. I have an awareness when it happens, give myself a moment of grace, and fall right back into my discipline.

I also no longer have a defeatist attitude toward certain necessary physical activities such as running or endurance biking; rather, I embrace these activities and enjoy the emotional and physical high they provide. You see, it is not just about the body but how you purify your mind through the discipline. And through the correct physical fitness routine, your mind becomes cleansed, and you no longer want to turn to unhealthy nutritional behaviors.

My point here is to show that habits take time to instill. You need to give yourself grace to fall out of your discipline but then jump back in. You cannot repair all your trauma and change your nutritional behavior overnight. This doesn't happen with one intervention or one plant medicine ceremony. It takes time, patience, and most of all, discipline.

Lastly, you should enjoy yourself. You are human; you can have days you loosen the rules and the belt, but don't let these days become habits. Practicing discipline when it comes to your nutritional behavior will lead to the healing of mind, body, soul, and any persisting ailments. Respect your body as the temple it is by giving it the right food and relaxation to have a deeper spiritual and healthier physical experience.

As my eating habits changed, I soon looked at many of the things I used to eat as poison or drugs. For example, when I used to go to the movies, I would love to get all sorts of "treats," but now I am content with water. I view what they serve as harmful to my energy and my spiritual, physical, and emotional well-being. Maybe one day they will offer healthier options at theaters, if they still exist. No one is saying do not enjoy yourself from time to time, but overindulgence with chemically compounded items is never a good choice.

Eating is not merely the intake of food, but the ritual intake of energy that can purify or toxify mind, body, and soul. It can either align you with the vibration of higher frequencies and divine consciousness, or you can become further entangled in unconscious desire, emotional imbalance, and egoic habit. You are what you eat.

Section 3 – Discipline your Senses to Purify Your Mind, Body and Soul Through Your Physical Fitness Routine

Overview

Your physical fitness routine is a major key into the discipline of your senses and ultimately the purification of your mind, body, and soul. Physical fitness keeps one's body in optimal working condition; it is an excellent stress and anxiety release and reconnects one to their breath. Through physical fitness, one can refine their sensory inputs and motor outputs, which send signals that shape our mental clarity, emotional stability, and spiritual alignment. Our posture, breath, and range of motion have a direct effect on the messages our senses send to our brain, creating either harmony or distortion in our inner world. As they say, movement is life.

Our physical fitness disciplines our senses as they must work in harmony and alignment to carry out the given activity. It is through this process that our body heals, our mind becomes calm, and our soul is purified. We can reconnect with our breath as we learn to breathe through moments of physical exertion and discomfort. This, in turn, trains us to regulate our breath, which aids us when we face obstacles in life that cause discomfort, fear, or anxiety.

While your physical fitness routine leads to the purification of your mind and soul, it starts with the body. The discipline of your senses through your physical fitness routine can be achieved by training for strength and muscle density, cardiovascular health, endurance, mobility and stability, and flexibility and recovery practices.

Our muscle tissue acts a s a metabolic organ; it supports hormone balance, insulin sensitivity, and resilience against physical stress. Training for strength and muscle density protects bone health, stabilizes joints, and prevents injury as you age. It is through strength training that we can physically ground ourselves in the day and increase our confidence. This has a direct impact on our mental attitude with ourselves and all those we encounter.

To ensure efficient oxygen delivery to the muscles and organs, we must train for cardiovascular health. Oxygen is the giver of life and allows our breath to function. When oxygen is properly flowing, we gain stability of our emotions and can regulate our automatic nervous system. When we are less anxious, we have greater discipline over our senses and can focus on attracting higher frequencies.

Endurance training teaches us patience, discipline, and the ability to sustain effort without burnout. It is through this type of training that we build resilience. We can endure more physically, spiritually, and emotionally as we increasingly push our physical endurance limits. This allows us to keep our mind purified, composed, and present when life is stressful and noisy.

It is through our stability training that we gain more awareness of our body and the space it is in, thus creating presence. It creates an awareness that we must be present in the moment and not live in the past or the future. Through this awareness, we gain greater discipline of our senses and our movement becomes a meditation. We move with fluidity, and our joints stay healthy and less stressed. A stable body leads to a stable mind.

Many of us know that when we become emotionally stressed, we also become tense. This tension is stored in our tissues. It is through activities like stretching, yoga, and breathwork that we can release this tension. These activities aid in our flexibility and recovery which prevent future injuries and support energetic flow, all for emotional release and spiritual openness. These activities also assist in moving and clearing stuck energy in the nadis and allow us to actively balance the energy in our chakra system.

Through rhythmic breathing and increased physical activity, our body can enter a flow state. It is our conscious breath that is the mechanism for both effort and recovery. Deep, rhythmic breathing sustains clarity and prevents fatigue during endurance training, while powerful, focused breath sharpens awareness and inner power during strength or high intensity training. It is through the mastery of our breath that our workouts become a purification ritual for our mind, body, and soul.

When we enter a flow state through physical fitness, our inner noise is silenced, we are no longer self-conscious, and we enter pure presence, a divine state of consciousness. It is in these moments we can find clarity about problems of the day that have perplexed us and cause us discomfort, pain, and suffering. We can come to terms with the fact that no obstacle is insurmountable, and we can alleviate any limiting beliefs. Physical fitness is a moving meditation that allows us to gain discipline over our senses, turn within, raise our vibration, reach for higher frequencies, and connect us to our divinity.

The Victim and Physical Fitness

The physical fitness routine of the victim is colored by pain and suffering. They feel it is a form of punishment that causes physical, emotional, and mental discomfort. It is the victim's mindset to believe that they cannot not achieve their goals as they are at the mercy of external forces such as age, genetics, and their environment.

When working out, their senses are undisciplined, and their mind receives signals of mental fatigue, muscle fatigue, exhaustion, and despair. They cannot control their breath and are constantly complaining of being winded and wounded. The victim will make physical and emotional excuses to avoid finishing or even beginning their physical fitness routine. They just don't see the point in it as they have no confidence that they can complete an activity or reach their desired goals.

In the Victim's mind, everyone else is better than them at all activities, so there is no point in making an effort or trying. They rather avoid training as it highlights their perceived weakness and inadequacy. They fail to recognize that the only person you are in competition with is yourself, to be more physically fit and healthier than the day before.

The victim would rather give up than try. They would rather admit defeat than risk failure and be embarrassed. Instead, they choose numbing activities like overeating, video games, social media, and watching TV. While these momentary dopamine hits bring temporary emotional relief, they also lead to a weaker mental state, lower confidence, and further physical and medical ailments. They fail to recognize that there is no failure with physical fitness; rather, it is the act of pushing through and giving it your best shot that makes all those that try winners.

The Survivor and Physical Fitness

The survivor recognizes that physical fitness is a tool to discipline their senses and regain control over their life and health. However, the survivor views their physical fitness routine through tracking accomplishments and wins. If they cannot boast about it, it might as well not have happened.

The survivor has learnt through failure, trial, and error that undisciplined senses lead to a deterioration of their physical fitness routine. They understand and have awareness that the foods, sounds, and images they take in through their senses can have a negative or positive affect on their workouts.

Unfortunately, some of their motivation still stems from fear of past events, fear of illness, fear of aging, and fear of regression. They are also motivated by competition and comparison, which can be good as it keeps one pushing for greater accomplishment, but it can also have a negative effect on the psyche if their benchmarks are not within their physical reach. The survivor likes to celebrate their victories, and during these times, they can fall out of their discipline, allowing their senses to become less discriminatory to the stimuli they absorb.

The survivor is goal-oriented with their physical fitness and likes to feel that there is a finish line to all modalities or a psychological medal they can win. Their physical fitness routine is used to prove their resilience to self and others. They strive to take consistent steps toward strength, endurance, and health, although imperfect due to their comparison to others for accomplishment and validation.

The Warrior and Physical Fitness

Through their physical fitness routine, the warrior gains control of their senses and turns within to cultivate light, love, and source energy. They warrior makes no excuses when it comes to physical fitness. They practice various modalities and make necessary modifications to their routine when necessary. This can be due to injuries, weather, location, and other externalities that are out of their control.

It is through their physical fitness routine that they gain complete control of their senses. Training is not just about appearance; rather, it sharpens their awareness and heightens their sensory control. During their physical fitness routine, they use their senses as tools in gaining breath control, mental clarity, and physical well-being. Their practice is a sacred discipline through which they purify and align their mind, body, and soul. It is a spiritual ritual to the warrior.

The warrior incorporates sense control, breathwork, and nutritional behaviors to aid them on their physical fitness journey. They know physical, nutritional, and emotional inputs have a direct correlation to their progress and do all within their power to stay in divine alignment with their environment and its stimuli.

The warrior knows the burn is the blessing. It is through the discomfort of their physical fitness routine that they forge themselves in the fire of life, eventually becoming the fire. They understand that physical fitness is a journey, not a destination. You can have goals and markers along your journey so you may continue to level up and push yourself further; however, there is no end to the journey. Your light just continues to grow brighter, illuminating and healing yourself and those you share this divine energy with along the way. Through their discipline and their physical fitness routine, they find their devotion to themselves and ultimately to divine consciousness. They become the light.

<u>My Journey and Finding One's Modalities</u>

One of the biggest challenges of disciplining your senses through your physical fitness routine is finding the modalities that work for you. The modality must align with the given set and setting of your life. These modalities can change based on where you live, your goals, your injuries, and your needs.

I always enjoyed being physical; however, it wasn't until later in life that I realized that I lacked discipline with my senses, and this was hindering the physical, emotional, and mental benefits I received from my activities. I don't ever feel I had a victim's mentality when it came to my physical fitness routine; however, I did have a survivor's mentality.

Let me tell you why I feel had a survivor mentality. I often would limit myself to various activities due to things I perceived as obstacles or limitations, like my physical weight. I didn't think I would be good a team sports, as I was slower and heavier than most. Also, being in the locker room exposed me to being picked on for my size, so rather than deal with this head on, I avoided it at all costs. I believe this is why I focused on individual activities most of my life.

As an adolescent, I loved roaming the neighborhood on my bike and in my teen years I began going to the gym religiously. I had a focus on weight training and cardiovascular work outs. However, my nutritional behavior was undisciplined. Your physical fitness routine and nutritional behavior go hand and hand. The fuel or poison you feed your senses either enhances your routine and recovery or harms it.

As life progressed, I began to pick up new modalities. Yoga became a staple in my routine starting at age twenty-eight. There are many forms of yoga, but my focus was and still is vinyasa flow. Vinyasa flow is where movement is synched to breathing. It is one of the more active forms of yoga. Yoga brought with it the warrior's mentality. Through my yoga practice, I began to dispel many of my limiting beliefs I had when it came to my fitness routine.

No matter what was going on in my life, I always made time for my physical fitness routine. I always understood it to be necessary for both my physical and mental well-being. As years passed, new modalities such as HIIT, or High Intensity Interval Training, were incorporated. I first learned about HIIT training when my friend Bill and his trainer intervened in my health story. While I still enjoy these workouts solo, there are now numerous classes and gyms built specifically around these modalities.

Sometimes, life is moving so fast that we are just going through the motions and not really practicing with awareness. This hinders our ability to reap the full benefits until something like the Covid Pandemic happens and the world as you know it ceases to exist.

Due to the lockdowns, I began running outside. I also started having a better awareness of what I ate. We were in a health war, both physically and mentally, and it was time to optimize my spiritual practice, my nutritional behavior, and my physical fitness routine.

I had been doing yoga for over a decade. Being that the gyms were closed, I began doing my own flows at home and at the beach. Through some friends I was made aware of a group that was conducting teacher trainings online, so I jumped right in for my 200 hour RYT certification. It gave me something to do during lockdown and provided community.

I immediately took to the training. Just as important as the sequencing was being able to dive deeply into the philosophy of yoga and Hindu tenants such as those found in the book *The Yoga Sutras of Patanjali*. I feel the yamas (restraints) and niyamas (observances) are primary tenants to my mental and emotional well-being as well as my relationship with self.

Lockdown was difficult time for all. It created dissonance between loved ones. It isolated people physically, emotionally, and mentally. Whether the actions taken by our government were right or wrong, they happened, and we are still unpacking the psychological effects. I only saw two options: to evolve or devolve.

It was through this process that I learned of the power behind your physical fitness routine. My physical fitness routine provided me the necessary structure to discipline my senses and purify my mind, body, and soul. My new behaviors soon became habits, and these habits continue to allow me to forge a better version of myself with each workout.

I found myself and my light through endurance biking, running, HIIT, strength training, and yoga. I gained a new version of myself, reconnected to breath, and was a better friend to myself and others.

Through my studies at this time, I also began to segment my workouts based on the benefits I needed to achieve. I am not talking about weight, but rather what workouts were going to satiate the necessary categories of strength and muscle density, cardiovascular health, endurance, mobility, stability, and flexibility and recovery practices. What collection of workouts were going to increase my healthspan?

Many people today speak about longevity but often fail to recognize that it encompasses both lifespan and healthspan. Lifespan refers to the total number of years one lives, while healthspan reflects the quality, vitality, and functional capacity of those years. Extending healthspan requires intentional action to prevent or delay the four primary categories of chronic disease responsible for most mortality in industrialized nations: atherosclerotic cardiovascular disease, cancer, neurodegenerative disease, and metabolic dysfunction. Central to this effort is physical fitness, as regular strength training, cardiovascular conditioning, and mobility-based movement support metabolic and cardiovascular health, preserve neuromuscular and cognitive function, and sustain independence, resilience, and overall quality of life across the lifespan.

It is through trial and error that we find our modalities for our physical fitness routine. And then it is through discipline, determination, and grit that we can refine our practice to optimize its purification of our mind, body, and soul. You cannot get discouraged, as some days you will feel like you are pushing a boulder up hill, but through your discipline you will not give up. And over time, you will find a flow state that synchs your breath to your mind and your mind to your soul. You won't need drugs, alcohol, or any other external substance to reach this state of higher frequencies; rather, you will reach higher frequencies through the alignment and purification of mind, body, and soul that is achieved through a regimented physical fitness routine. No excuses.

Section 4 – Discipline your Senses to Purify Your Mind, Body, and Soul Through Your Relationship with Self and Others

Discipline your Eyes – How you see yourself and others

Overview

Our eyes give birth to our vision. They are the gateway of the world we live in and what we believe to be true. They shape thoughts in your mind about people, places, and things we encounter on our journey, yet most people do not practice discipline in what they allow themselves to see.

Rather, we stare without discipline into all forms of media that we have access to and scenery that appears in our site. Whether it is through social media, the news, videogames, movies, TV, or just our immediate environment, we let our eyes wander at scenes that have both high and low frequencies, and then we wonder why many have a depressed, gloomy, anxiety-ridden outlook on the world, ourselves, and our environment. Simple: you have been feeding your eyes poison.

Put another way, think of how you feel when you stare into nature or in the direction of someone that you have love for, whether they be a companion, close friend, or family member. One will see they have feelings of calmness, love, power, safety, elevation, and possibly oneness. These are all energies that are associated with higher states of consciousness and higher frequencies. And one would come to see upon a muscle test, through behavioral kinesiology, that they would physically test strong.

Behavioral kinesiology is a branch of applied kinesiology that explores how muscle responses reflect emotional, mental, and behavioral states. It's based on the premise that the body—specifically muscle strength—can reveal subconscious beliefs, stress responses, and imbalances in the nervous system. You can read more about this in the book *Your Body Doesn't Lie* by John Diamond M.D., who is credited with developing the modality.

Now let's think about the way one might feel when they are doom scrolling and have no filter on what they see coming across their smart phone, or when one sees a horrific accident or negative news story. Most people would say they feel anxious, scared, upset, or even downright sick. These are all emotions associated with lower states of consciousness, or lower frequencies. And one would come to see upon a muscle test, through behavior kinesiology, that they physically would test weak.

As the saying goes, if it bleeds, it leads. Through our social feeds and traditional media, we can be drawn to images that cause us pain and suffering. Wars, school shootings, and homelessness are everywhere we turn these days. And with the advent of streaming services over the last twenty years, fictional programming has become more graphic and negative than ever before. And for some reason, we can't look away; we choose the momentary high or dopamine hit and disregard the long-term harm we are doing to our psyche by not practicing discipline with our eyes.

By no means am I saying don't watch streaming services or don't use social media, but if we practice discipline with our eyes, we can selectively manage images that uplift us and not bring us down. No one is going to stop using their eyes for enjoyment, and whether it's movies, news, television shows, social media or video games, you are bound to partake in consumption of some low frequency imagery. But we must be mindful of the frequency or number of hours where we devote our attention to negative images and make sure we're giving our eyes the positive sustenance they need.

We must do a better job at consuming content. It can be helpful to watch things that elevate our consciousness such travel shows, shows on art, concerts, shows on spiritualty, or any other mind-elevating experience. We need discipline so our eyes do not take in images that cause mental and emotional harm.

It is understandable that we consume so much content; we want to stay up to date with current events, or we want a good spook by watching a thriller or a drama, but nonetheless, we are poisoning our minds. Over the last few years, I have made it a point to limit my exposure to negative images. I especially stay away from anything that has negative overtones visually prior to sleep as this can have detrimental effects on my subconscious.

Having discipline with your eyes has a direct emotional effect on your state of physical, emotional, mental, and spiritual well-being, which is why it is important to understand that just because you have eyes doesn't mean you should take in all the images that come your way. You must cultivate the discipline of being discerning with your eyes to avoid negative visual inputs when possible.

How you interpret images through your eyes will have either a detrimental or beneficial effect on your mind, body, and soul. Now, we understand that some things are unavoidable, but it is a choice to continue to stare at a negative image. Rather, one might just say a prayer for those involved in the image and practice non-attachment to the visual stimulation and let it pass.

How you use your eyes has a direct correlation of the purity of your mind as it relates to our relationship with self and others. Your eyes are a window into your soul. How I see myself, how I see my loved ones, and how I see my business partners can either lead to negative frequencies or positive frequencies. How we see these people in our lives will determine the outcome of the relationship, whether it be business or personal.

Your Drishti in yoga studies is where you choose to focus your gaze, but it can also be further interpreted as what outlook you have on things. This comes down to how you process the images and scenery that you are a party to, and whether you can find positivity in all things you meet visually. This is not always possible, but having a positive mental attitude will shape the way you view things that are happening around you and to you. How you choose to process visual stimuli will shape whether your experience is a lesson, a healing, a blessing, a curse, or a burden.

To expand on this, if the frequencies you are emitting are anger, fear, or anxiety, then you will process all images that come in with these emotions. Conversely, if the frequencies you are emitting are love, understanding, compassion, empathy, and acceptance, then these emotions will be used to process things that you visually see. A positive mental attitude toward the external world will aid in your growth and making sure that scenery doesn't give way to negative mindstuff.

Discipline with your eyes also means how we project our feelings and emotions through them to those we meet. If we are not careful, we can communicate things through our eyes that can be unfriendly or harmful in our interaction with other people. This then causes the receiving party to become defensive or standoffish. What you say with your eyes can either lead to a positive or negative initial meeting with someone prior to any words being spoken, and following through the length of the interaction. Our relationship with others is partially determined, and in many cases initially determined, on how we communicate with them with our eyes.

We want to use our eyes and bear witness to the miraculous power of the universe that unfolds before us. Our eyes are the portal to witness consciousness and shape the view we have on our environment and how we interact with it. We must also learn to cultivate and practice non-attachment to things we visually encounter. Remember, it is not what you see that causes pain, anger, or discomfort, but rather what you THINK you see, the story the mind has created as it attached emotions and past experiences, such as trauma, to the visual.

The Victim and Their Eyes

The victim will choose to color all images they see with negative emotions. They will search for negative news over their social media, streaming media, and traditional news outlets. This can be seen on their social media algorithms. Seeing other people go through negative experiences helps the victim feel a sense of belonging and comfort.

The victim looks through the world with a distorted gaze. They see the world through the lens of pain, fear, and injustice. They attach negative meaning to images, believing life is happening to them and that they have no control or that they are out of control. Their inner vision is colored by the past, and their seeing is clouded by fear, shame, or self-doubt.

Subconsciously, they search for confirmation of their suffering, often attracting or noticing only what reinforces their wounds, pain, and suffering. They are unable to let go of the past, and this clouds their vision. Divine consciousness and Divine Presence are invisible to their perception; rather, they are looking for what is damaged and broken.

The Survivor and Their Eyes

The survivor sees the world through the lens of a first responder. They expect bad things to happen and are looking for ways to find a positive outcome. They do not turn away from negative images; rather, they are looking for resolution. It is not all bad as they communicate a message of resilience and determination with their eyes. Their eyes say they have been through a great deal, but they continue to carry on.

The survivor practices a selective gaze and sees both pain and progress, but they still have an issue practicing non-attachment and remain attached to the duality. They are looking to navigate, fight, or fix all things they encounter in the world. When they observe another, they see them as a threat, ally, or a benchmark. They are seeing the world through their own ego and are looking for validation, recognition, or signs of progress. The survivor feels they need to protect themselves from the world and their eyes communicate this defensive posture. They have an awareness of divine consciousness, but they have yet to trust in it and all it presents to them on their journey toward enlightenment.

The Warrior and Their Eyes

The warrior sees the light in all images. They look for the lesson in all experiences of life and refrain from focusing on scenes of pain and despair or interpreting them in this manner. The Warrior sees the world through the eyes of love. While they understand there is pain, poverty, and problems, they choose to look at how today is better than yesterday. They have discipline in the messages they communicate to others with their eyes.

The warrior gaze is pure. They understand that all things carry a message and the energy of the divine and that is what they see in them. No matter how painful the image may be, they know there is divine consciousness within it, and that it has arrived in their view with purpose and teaching. In some manner, even the most painful sites will bring meaning and light to their journey. Their gaze is filled with stoicism, equanimity, and love; it is soft, steady, and free of negative projection.

The warrior views themselves and others without judgment and lets go of images as quickly as they arrive. Their vision is steady and calm no matter how big the waves of life might become. They know all things are part of one divine consciousness, and there is no separation from the divine, only unity, and this is how they view all things that come into their sight line. They view the world through the eyes of pure love without the want of reciprocity, without judgment, and this is what their eyes communicate with all they encounter.

My Journey to Discipline My Eyes

Through my eyes, my desires can be given strength and lead to negative behavior in the mundane world. What I see affects my behavior and attitude toward others and myself. Growing up, I loved to watch gangster movies; I still can recite lines from *King of New York*, *Goodfellas*, *Casino*, and *Heat*. However, as I grew older, I realized that while I could enjoy these movies, I needed to not desire the lifestyles being emulated. It is hard to tell a teenager or young adult to turn away from the opulence depicted in these movies of money, power, respect, and sex.

While you watch movies like this, or as some may play first person shooter video games or take in any other similar negative images, your eyes become desensitized, and you desire similar things. The lifestyle of these characters appealed to me, and my desires would take control in social settings, minus the violence. My attitude would emulate the characters I watched in these movies. I was allowing my eyes to create unwanted desires and aggressive attitudes. I still enjoy these types of movies in moderation, but I no longer allow my desires to get in entangled in the story line. I am not saying you shouldn't enjoy things in moderation, but you must find balance and limit the negative imagery.

Porn is another major issue that stimulates unhealthy desires in people of all ages. Sexuality is a wonderful thing; it is an exchange of energy, of life force, between people that can produce higher frequencies. I was never addicted to porn, but I enjoyed watching it from time to time until I realized it was causing intimacy issues in my relationships and issues with my thoughts around monogamy.

My eyes were overexposed to situations that I feel are unhealthy, spiritually and emotionally. I am not passing judgment on anyone here; I am speaking for myself. Sexuality is thrown at us from every direction these days, and you need to make sure you are not allowing your eyes to desire things that are detrimental to your relationship with your loved one.

Our sexual energy is our life force, our prana, and when you partake in activities that drain it, you are giving your lifeforce away without it being replenished. When I started thinking about it this way, I began to question the effect viewing porn had on my sexual behavior and stopped watching it all together. I choose to reserve this energy for my partner and no one else.

I still have difficulty keeping negative images from entering my eyes through social media. The algorithms know which issues we are most emotional about, and content providers know the more dramatic the post, the more engagement they will achieve. I have found it especially difficult to keep negative messaging away from my eyes with respect to the current political climate.

However, I am becoming more aware of the negative impact it has on my psyche, so I am quicker to unfollow accounts that sensationalize the current pain and suffering in the world. The algorithms on social media will have you feeling negative emotions towards your friends and family and have you loving your enemy. You should embrace support and uplift the ones who are righteous and just, which means understanding that many of these feeds/posts are looking to incite you to engage you in the story/drama.

I make it a point to not open my social media feeds until the first three hours of my morning routine are accomplished. This allows me to set the tone of my day with positivity, gratitude, and love. When I do engage with my social feeds, I have a greater awareness, and I am able to pause and pivot when I begin to doom scroll or when the algorithm is pushing negative feedback loops.

Social media wants people to take sides, to judge, to criticize, but we are all divine consciousness. You must close your eyes to this noise and "real eyes" that you should have love, compassion, and empathy for all you encounter. And when you do perceive negativity and destruction, you should send blessings rather than aggression and hate. We should be looking for the center and speaking into understanding and resolution. Most people are not as far apart in their beliefs as the pundits would have you believe.

How do I see myself in the mirror? What story am I telling myself, how have been programmed to see myself and others? How has it had a negative or positive affect on my day, my relationships, my life, and my journey? What can I do to actively correct how I see myself?

Anyone who has body image issues can attest that looking in the mirror can be hard and painful. At times, I still see someone with weight issues in in the mirror, someone who has and can let their insecurities rule how they react to people and situations. This has had a detrimental effect on my behavior in personal and business situations and has cost me friends and business deals.

I realized on my journey that seeing myself this way was a slippery slope. Through my own eyes I was passing negative judgement on myself, and when I did so, it became easier to speak to myself negatively about where I was at in life, both personally and professionally. It also affected my empathy and compassion for others as it became easier to criticize and judge them for their behavior and actions.

Through my own eyes, I shamed myself when I looked in a mirror. I lacked discipline. I needed to change because I am the first person I see in the morning and the last one I see when I go to sleep. If my day begins and ends with a negative conversation with myself, then everything in between will carry negative overtones as well. I will speak negatively to those I encounter, and all situations will be viewed through these negative glasses.

In the past, I would show up to both business and personal meetings with eyes that communicated this negativity. Failures of past business deals colored my vision. What-ifs and could-have-beens shaped the backdrop of my vision. My eyes told those around me that I was angry, judgmental, and ready to react without listening. This created unnecessary obstacles in creating relationships and a positive container for interactions with others.

Through my own journey, I realized that something as simple as looking in the mirror and seeing myself in a positive light could have a beneficial effect on my mental well-being. To purify my mind, I needed to practice discipline in seeing myself.

Now, when I show up, I do so with soft and welcoming eyes. I create a safe space for myself and others before words even exit my mouth through my eyes. Rather than communicating turmoil and pain, my eyes communicate safety, openness, empathy, and compassion.

I still find myself being critical of the person I see in the mirror, but when I do, I fall into my discipline. I embody the warrior. I know how far I have come spiritually, mentally, physically, and emotionally, and I no longer carry the bags of shame for who I was, as I am work in progress. And I realize what I see in front of me is the light; it is part of divine consciousness. Now I ask you, how do you see yourself? Are you setting yourself up for success or failure when you look in the mirror?

Our eyes should not be used without discipline. They should provide clarity on our journey to enlightenment. You must choose to look at things in a positive light, as positive lessons. Do not add negative emotions to the interpretation of what you see. Negative emotions only lead to attachment, pain, suffering, and the inability to let go, ultimately stunting our spiritual growth. You must not allow your desires to let you behave in a low frequency manner, yearning for things that others have or that you think you are owed. You must learn which desires are in line with your journey to enlightenment, thus making the realization that you are in control of your desires and your desires shouldn't control you.

As we vibrate higher, toward Higher Frequencies, we want to move toward non-attachment. We want to release labels from things we see and not pass judgment on whether they are good or bad, which can lead to the wrong overall mindset and point of view. We want to desire less and love more. We want to let go of what no longer serves our higher state of being.

This is the why it is important to practice discipline with your eyes, as that through this discipline we can purify the way we see ourselves, others, and the world, leading to a more fulfilling and joy filled life.

<u>Discipline your Ears – How you listen to yourself and others</u>

<u>Overview</u>

What we allow into our ears has a direct impact on the emotional environment we create internally and externally. The frequencies we allow in affect our mind and can put us in a low or high frequency state of being. Let's dive into how the sounds, speeches, and combination of words we allow to enter our ears affects our well-being and outlook on the environment and the people we encounter.

In one aspect, we will focus on what we allow to enter our ears and how sounds and combination of words that we allow in can either raise or lower our vibration. In another aspect, we must give the proper attention and focus to someone who is communicating with us. If one is sharing energy in the form of sound, whether that be speech, words or music, we want to make sure we are receptive, respectful, patient, and open.

As we move toward Higher Frequencies, we want to ensure the words and sounds we listen to vibrate at the frequencies that purify our mind, body, and soul. The words we listen to and the sounds we hear all carry energy. If we are not careful, what we listen to can shape a world of fear, anxiety, and depression. Watching negative movies and shows, listening to music that doesn't carry positive messages or frequencies, or listening to the doom and gloom of the news can all have a detrimental effect on our overall mental and emotional well-being. We should focus on positive messaging, music, and sounds which uplift our energy and provide enlightenment in the messaging.

We must be realistic and understand we cannot always prevent negative sounds from entering our space. When practicing discipline with our ears, we must remember that not every opinion is meant for your ears and meant for you, especially when it is of low frequency and sparks emotions of fear, doubt, shame, or anger. It is a good rule of thumb to focus and listen to sounds and words that ignite your heart with positive energy.

A great way to counterbalance some of the negative sounds that might be taken in is to take a walk and listen to nature or listen to high-vibrational music. We can also have a conversation with a friend about an uplifting subject matter or one of healing and resolution. Through awareness of our intake with our ears, we can find balance and harmony in our day.

A great tool to cleanse and purify any impurities we encounter through our ears is via mantra repetition. A mantra is a scared message, text, or sound that vibrates at higher frequencies. It is one of the best purifying modalities one can use and tap into, no matter the time or place.

Mantra repetition is helpful for mediation and for times when our mind starts talking to us in a negative manner. At these times, we can pause and turn to a mantra or affirmation to drown out negative thoughts. Words and sounds that enter the ears influence the heart both emotionally and physically.

When we practice discipline with our ears, we can become anchored in the sounds of truth. This leads to divine confidence, and divine connection with oneself and consciousness. We do not want our frequencies to become polluted by listening to things that do not serve us or sounds and words that disconnect us from our highest selves and higher frequencies.

We often multitask on our smartphones and become distracted when someone communicating with others. However, we must practice discipline with our ears when another person is communicating with us. It is important to make eye contact and listen with discipline as their words can have an uplifting effect on our mood and energy. Giving someone your full attention can raise our vibration, and conversely, trying to listen to many things at once is not only disrespectful to the other party, but depletes our energy and vibe.

On the path to higher frequencies, the way we listen becomes a sacred discipline. Listening is more than a passive act—it is an energetic choice. What we allow into our field through sound directly impacts our consciousness, our nervous system, and our ability to remain attuned to truth.

Disciplining the sense of hearing means teaching our ears to seek what uplifts. We must listen for what enhances vitality, calms the mind, and purifies the soul. Every sound we absorb is either strengthening or weakening our inner frequencies. The sounds we take in are either cleansing or polluting our energy channels and centers.

Remember, you are not required to receive sounds and words that are abusive or harmful. If someone speaks from anger, negativity, projection, or fear, we can simply decline to let that sound penetrate. Think of someone offering you a gift or piece of food that you do not want; you can politely turn it down. You can do the same with negative words and sounds. Absorbing verbal abuse—whether once or repeatedly—slowly hardens the heart. It blocks our capacity to forgive, to love deeply, and to feel our own goodness. We are not here to accept frequencies that do harm to our emotional and mental well-being.

Part of rising in consciousness and in vibration is refusing to engage with the voices of those who distort truth or radiate low vibrations. This includes your own inner voice which can be your own worst energy. When we listen to the opinions of those rooted in toxicity, confusion, or perversion, we erode our inner clarity. Over time, this dulls our ability to discern truth from noise.

Conversely, when we open our ears to affirming words, to sacred teachings, and to those who see the divine in us, we activate new energy within that uplifts and heals. We build stamina, joy, and purpose. We become more available to serve humanity from a place of fullness. We hear divine consciousness in all things.

Sound itself is medicine. Mantras, drumming, sacred music, and chanting awaken the body's subtle energy centers. They purify the sense of hearing, repair the nervous system, and restore the natural rhythm of the soul. These vibrations touch chakras, unblock energetic pathways (nadis), and raise our entire system into coherence, balance, and equanimity.

Even the act of listening to sacred chants carries transformative power. These sounds refine the auditory field, calm the mind, and draw us deeper into alignment with truth and higher frequencies. Eventually, listening becomes an act of devotion, the mind quiets completely, and what remains is stillness, presence, and the resonance of divine consciousness.

This is the practice discipline of with your ears. It's a return to intentionality in sound. A reclaiming of our inner vibrational landscape. And it is one of the most direct ways we elevate ourselves, one frequency at a time.

The Victim and Their Ears

The victim listens through their wounds. They hear the world through their own negative inner noise, manifesting the of voice of pain, anxiety, fear, judgment, shame and hopelessness. They do not let go of the past and therefore are never truly in the present.

They find comfort and belonging in listening to negative news, music, and media. The negativity affirms their personal reality of pain and suffering. They prefer to engage in conversation that speaks into their negative beliefs and fear.

We all have that friend, business colleague, or family member who we offer advice to, but they respond as if they are constantly being attacked. This is a victim mentality. They lean into their suffering, and this prevents them from hearing divine consciousness and the sound of unconditional love.

When a friend, family member, or spiritual leader tries to correct the victim, all they hear is rejection. They misinterpret the message through their own ego and pain. You can see this manifest in their physical body as their breath is shallow and they are constantly distracted. This prevents them from hearing not only others, but their soul's voice as well.

The victim doesn't have faith or trust in a higher power. They question whether there is a higher power. They stop listening and therefore cannot hear divine consciousness. This completely separates them from the spiritual realm, and they find themselves landlocked in the mundane world. They are their ego; they are one in the same.

The Survivor and Their Ears

The survivor hears more clearly as they have risen above low frequency emotions such as shame and guilt; however, they still listen through filters of ego or self-preservation. They still carry fear and anxiety of the possibilities of new trauma occurring.

They selectively hear what confirms their progress or justifies their control; however, they ignore anything that challenges their point of view as their ego views it as an attack.

The ego hijacks spiritual teachings for personal identity; it keeps us trapped in the Maya, Illusion or delusionary state of this world. A goal of spiritual enlightenment is dissolution of the ego, which can take a lifetime or even multi-life journey. This is understood by many of the great faiths; spiritual enlightenment cannot be fully achieved until our soul transitions to divine consciousness.

Maya is the concept we started to discuss earlier; it is the illusionary or delusionary state our physical body and ego live in. This is created when the soul returns to the body for this physical incarnation. One might say the soul has amnesia and forgets it is a part of divine consciousness; rather, it becomes attached to the physical body of this incarnation. The illusion or delusion is further colored through ego and egos' interaction with our senses and the world around us. The greater the ego, the greater the delusion. It is the goal of meditation to shut down the sense telephones, turn within, reconnect to the divine, and know that we are all one energy.

While the survivor is devoted to spiritual growth, often their pride becomes a hinderance to hearing things without judgment. They will listen to their friends, loved ones, and spiritual leaders, but in most cases, they are looking for validation and are not looking to be challenged. They will not really hear them when they are speaking. One might say they have selective hearing; they engage the techniques but may use them to validate, achieve, or conquer rather than to surrender.

When we listen to others, we need to be open to change our point of view with new facts and information. When we already are searching for a predetermined outcome, listening becomes goal-oriented, as with the Survivor, and is not as effective as it could be. They have faith, but their trust is shaky—so they listen to voice of divine consciousness but do not always have patience necessary to allow the timing to unfold.

The Warrior and Their Ears

The warrior listens with openness, humility, and stillness. The warrior listens with their heart even when it might cause momentary pain. They listen with love even when being attacked, as they understand this a projection of the persons' trauma. However, they do not allow the sounds to cause any suffering. As they saying goes, pain is inevitable in life; however, suffering is a choice. Suffering is the output of not practicing letting go and non-attachment.

The warrior chooses to limit their listening to music, talk, and media that uplifts their emotional and spiritual well-being. When a negative conversation or interaction begins, they are quick to disengage. They limit their exposure to the news cycle and stay clear of music that speaks into death, destruction, negativity, and things such as misogyny. The Warrior is aware of the negative programming that society would like to impose on them and how it can impede their spiritual journey. They are not interested in "getting with the program" or "getting on the train."

The warrior purifies any inner noise through the practice of non-attachment and letting go. They no longer listen to react—they listen to receive. Whether from God, Guru, another human, or life itself, every sound becomes a sacred transmission. Each sound is used as guidance on their journey toward enlightenment, and the goal is to hear the light and follow its hum.

The warrior hears the spiritual leaders' words as nectar, as direct communion with divine consciousness. Even silence becomes instruction. In the context of Higher Frequencies, nectar symbolizes the profound sweetness and divine grace that arises when the soul connects deeply with its higher self and the divine consciousness. It is the subtle, blissful essence experienced during moments of spiritual awakening, meditation, or inner stillness—like a gentle flow of light and love that nourishes and uplifts the mind, body, and spirit. This nectar is not physical but energetic, a taste of the divine that transcends ordinary perception, reminding us of our innate purity and connection to Source. Experiencing this nectar invites a shift into higher vibrational states, where healing, clarity, and expanded awareness naturally unfold.

In deep meditation, the warrior listens for *Nada*, the inner sound current. Their listening is subtle, devotional, and intuitive. The warrior hears divine consciousness not just in prayer, but in the wind, in suffering, in silence. The warrior knows the sound of the divine is omnipresent, we are it and it is us, and that it must be embodied.

<u>My journey to Discipline My Ears</u>

Listening to others has always been a challenge for me. I am not talking about taking direction from others, although that is challenging to me as well, but rather giving someone my attention and following their words. While I hear all the words they are saying, I didn't always listen.

I feel that hearing and listening are two different things. Hearing someone speak and being able to tell them verbatim what they just said is not listening. Listening, to me, means not over speaking or cutting someone off while they are speaking to you. It means being present to the conversation and not just waiting for them to finish so you may say what is on your mind or give your response.

In my personal and business life, this has been challenging. My mind works extremely fast, and I can hear someone, but at the same time, can be jumping to a conclusion and waiting to say my peace or point of view. I also had, and sometimes still have, the tendency to over speak others. This is not only rude but also creates dissonance when you are having a conversation and looking to find resonance and resolution in both personal and business matters.

However, I am getting much better at listening to others. I make sure to take several breaths during a conversation as well as take a moment to breathe a few times after the person has stopped, making sure they are not just at a pause but rather at the end of their train of thought. Through this process, I not only hear the words, but I arrive and listen to the meaning and the intent.

All communication to me is negotiation, at the most basic level, and it is a negotiation for time and to be heard. By listening to others with disciplined ears, we raise the vibration of the conversation as all parties feel a part of the frequency and are in resonance rather than dissonance.

One of the hardest aspects of practicing discipline with our ears is listening to yourself and recognizing the voice that is guiding you on your journey. For many of us, the noise of our minds, the constant chatter, the mindstuff, can be overbearing. Who in our head is speaking to us? Is it our ego, is it our trauma, is it our insecurities, or is it our higher self? We take in some much external stimuli; we can be overwhelmed by our mindstuffs' analysis. It can become difficult to know what to listen to and what to ignore.

This is where mediation and prayer come in. When we meditate or pray, and we will get into the difference later in the book, we give the mind the opportunity to disconnect from the external world. It is through meditation and prayer that we can listen closely to divinity in us and what it is suggesting about a given situation.

You can also discipline what enters your ears and psyche through finding your flow state. On its most basic level, flow state is a return to your breath, your lifeforce, your prana. While psychedelics aid in this process, we should note that the actual medicine is your breath itself. Many of us are rushing around in life that our breathing becomes unbalanced and shallow. It is our breath that is our life force aka our prana. We can arrive back at our breath and in flow state naturally through meditation and physical activity such as running, swimming, biking, walking, cross-fit, and yoga.

There are also breathing techniques such as a box breathing, and we will talk about this more later as well, to calm our nervous system and allow us to hear internal voice. The most notable form of breathing techniques is Holotropic breathwork.

Holotropic breathwork was developed by Stanislav Grof, a Czech psychiatrist, and his wife in response to LSD being made illegal. They had been doing therapeutic studies with LSD as a catalyst for healing in their patient sessions. However, once made illegal, they could no longer provide this treatment.

Through their previous studies, they noticed a breathing pattern emerge when the patients were under the effects of the medicine. Over the course of the next few years and refinement of the process, the Groff's were able induce a psychedelic experience without LSD or any other external substances. This was done through a rhythmic breathing cadence and the use of various music, some tribal, some modern, that followed a similar cadence. It was an exercise in breath and listening with one's ears.

The patient's rhythmic breathing patterns elevated them to a state of divinity, bringing their mundane world to the spiritual realm without external substances, just with breath. When we return to our breath, we can hear ourselves with clarity and receive downloads from source energy. This is, to me, practicing discipline in listening.

Let's dive deeper in how music can harm or heal. Music has always been a part of my life. It is a bond I share with my family and most notably my father. My father began taking me to concerts when I was five. I cherished our weekly trips to buy tapes and CD's and our shared enjoyment of the music. We continue this day to share new music with each other, but it wasn't until the last decade that I realized I wasn't practicing discipline when it came to the music I listened too.

The realization came to me that lyrics are mantras, and when we listen to music and sing along, we are calling into our life the energy of that song. For example, if the lyrics are about love and healing, that is what we are calling in, but if the music is of low frequency and the lyrics are about crime, drug abuse, or derogatory to others, then that is the energy we are calling in.

Most of the music I grew up on was based in healing, love, knowledge of self, and mind elevation. However, I did listen to my fair share of negative music. I now practice discipline in listening with respect to the music I allow in my ears. Negative frequencies and lyrics have no place in my ears, and thankfully, I derive no enjoyment from them. You must ask yourself, what are you calling into existence through the music you listen to?

Unfortunately, much like the news, music that is negative is a main part of "the program." Lyrics that glorify materialism, destruction, disrespect to oneself and others, crime, and drug abuse are ever present in the mainstream and lead many of the charts on digital streams. That is why it is of utmost importance to practice discipline when choosing the music you listen to; it is something many of us don't think of.

We hear a catchy beat and start singing along because the song is showing up on all our streaming services, and next thing you know we are calling into action dark energy and dark forces. By listening to negative music, we are not only harming ourselves but giving strength to this negative energy spectrum and all we encounter.

We must think of music like food for the ears. You wouldn't eat something tasty if you knew it was rotting you from within or causing physical health issues. Therefore, you shouldn't listen to music that sounds good but is causing spiritual and emotional harm and lowering your vibration.

Our ears are naturally outward-seeking and indiscriminate— they're drawn to absorb everything around them. We are misusing this sacred sense when we consistently listen to sounds, words, or energies that don't attract higher frequencies or assist us on our journey to enlightenment. Over time, this leads to energetic exhaustion and weakens the body's natural defenses, leaving us more vulnerable to stress, anxiety, imbalance, and even illness.

Practicing discipline with our ears helps preserve our vitality. It cultivates a calmer mind, deepens patience, and creates space between stimulus and reaction. And always remember: the Universe is listening. Be mindful of what you project—and equally mindful of what you allow in.

Discipline your Mouth – How you speak to yourself and others

Overview

We are more powerful than we think. And the sooner we realize that, the sooner we can manifest our dreams through our actions and our behaviors. The source, the divine, is always listening to our words. And we must remember that our word is our wand. Our words communicate to the universe our deepest wishes, wants, and unfortunately our fears and limiting beliefs. Our words put forth a chain of events that can be positive or negative.

It is of utmost importance that we choose our words wisely and with intention to manifest the life we want and deserve.

Our words are creative forces, whether we look at this from a scientific or mystical tradition. Words are infused with divine energy and manifest the life we live. They can shape the emotional field of relationships. Words carry frequencies and therefore can modify our vibrational state, calling in both low and higher frequencies depending on the words we use and the tone and context they are said in. Words are affirmations that can enforce both negative and positive self-beliefs and can establish either a negative view or positive view of oneself. Words can pollute or purify our mind. Speech is a spiritual act, and we must practice discipline when speaking to others and when speaking to ourselves.

Let's start by addressing self-talk, as this can either set you up for failure or success. Self-talk projects your feelings about yourself and your situation into the universe. One must be careful not to speak words of failure, despair, or negativity. Doing so creates a negative self-image of oneself and has oneself leaning into negative emotions. In essence, negative self-talk is asking the universe for more pain, suffering, and misgivings.

Negative self-talk is like being on a hamster wheel running in circles; it will never take you anywhere just make you feel drained, depleted, and exhausted. Rather through positive affirmations, even during difficult times, we can keep pushing forward toward our destiny. Instead of speaking negatively to yourself, when times are difficult, ask yourself what lessons can be learned from the current situation and what application can be used to forward my pursuit for personal and business success.

What blessings can I see when I unpack what I thought was a curse? Keep the conversation with yourself positive, forward moving, and uplifting.

We must also remember that it's not just the verbal expression of words that causes the universe to react, but also how we are speaking internally to ourselves. We are human, after all, and there are going to be times where we find ourselves spiraling into negative thoughts and wanting to vocalize negative energy. An overactive mind that falls into negative speech can be redirected into positivity through several facets. Engaging in physical activity, such as running, working out, and yoga, can help reframe the conversation with oneself and others into a positive light. Physical activity creates endorphins and activates our endocannabinoid system, taking us into a more positive state of being.

When it comes to speaking with others, we waste energy trying to convince the other party to see it our way or by talking in circles. When one is aware that their words have power, you realize you don't want to just speak the first thing that comes to mind. Doing so can lead to an energy depletion of all parties involved. This is especially true when your speech lacks concentration or contemplation.

You must contemplate before speaking. If we pause and pick which words need to be projected, we not only can bring the situation to center verbally but we can also inject the situation with positivity and forward momentum. Take a moment to make sure the words selected and the tone expressed is going to move the conversation in a positive direction and not cause disruption, dissonance, or negativity. Be sure to choose words that promote resolution. Our words and how we use them direct the universe to deliver positive or negative momentum. Through word play we decide and drive which one to fuel.

It needs to be restated that through our speech we create roots of manifestation. The vibration of our speech and the words that compose it bring things into existence. I am not just referring to the words themselves here, but also the tone and inflection in our voice. The lower the frequency you speak in, the more subject you will be to negative emotions.

We must be careful not to speak into negative messaging as it becomes engraved in our mind, our speech, and our reality. As discussed in discipline with our ears, this is especially true in the lyrics of the music we listen to, as that when we sing along with our favorite song, we are projecting, speaking, those lyrics into the universe. If the lyrics are destructive and melancholy, than we shouldn't be surprised when negative circumstances continue to come into our reality.

Other methods to purify speech are through mantra repetition, prayer, reciting sacred texts, indigenous chants, and listening to music with positive messaging. Through all these modalities we can not only cleanse our energy, but we can also lean into developing the set and setting we would like to manifest in our reality. You must ensure that in any of these methods, we choose words that are uplifting, positive, and strengthening.

You should choose to focus on things that bring light and love into your heart. By focusing on this thought and how it makes you feel, you can recalibrate your emotional response to what might be jarring you in the moment. If you remember that, the obstacle is the way you can look at challenges as learning experiences and speak positivity into your reaction to any occurrence. This not only changes your perspective now in time, but it also signals to the universe that you are learning and growing, and you are accepting of only positive energy in your life. If you can respond to the obstacles that present themselves in your life with love, hope, and optimism, the universe will respond accordingly.

We must practice discipline when we communicate with the divine, the source, the universe. Energy manifestation is real; you need to ask yourself what energy my words are calling into being, as like attracts like. Using the proper words will lead to the elevation of your energy and purification of your mind, body, and soul.

When we talk without thinking, our energy becomes depleted. We call into life situations that are negative which deters us on our journey to enlightenment. When you speak aloud or to yourself, you must make sure to use words with discrimination, concentration, and contemplation. This will keep your energy positive, and those things you attract positive as well, thus, leading to the manifestation of your dreams into your reality.

The Victim and Their Mouth

When you are living in your trauma and playing the victim, all of your speech is negative in nature. You are always on the defense. You speak to yourself in the voice of pain, powerlessness, and unworthiness. Even when those around you are supportive, you snap back with negative words. If you hear everything as an attack, then it is natural that you may want to attack back.

You may also just feel so beaten down that the words you chose to use are one of self-loathing and suffering. Victims enjoy expressing to others how hard their life is and how the odds are stacked up against them. They talk into their pain with anyone that will listen and anyone they encounter repeating stories of trauma, blame, and limiting beliefs. They tend to gossip, complain, and be pessimistic. In doing so, they call more discomfort into their life. They fail to ever recognize that, viewed differently, their misgivings are their greatest teachers and are part of their soul's correction.

In conversation with themselves, they are also self-loathing. They have tendency to say derogatory things to themselves. Victims are their own worst enemy. They talk themselves out of opportunity, prosperity, and love as they feel they are non-deserving of it. Their speech calls in low frequency fields of shame, guilt, and fear. One may consider their self-talk to be self-abuse.

The victim fails to recognize that negative speech disturbs your nervous system and your spiritual clarity. It is speech like this that lacks mindfulness and causes suffering to self and others. The world we live in is and was created by speech, and speech like this destroys and does not build positivity. The victim forgets their sacred responsibility to heal themselves and heal others, and it is most evident in their speech patterns.

The Survivor and Their Mouth

We all know the people who love to tell their story of their struggle and how they have persevered through life. The survivor wants all to know how much they have had to endure and continue to endure to be where they are in life. They hold on to their pain and suffering to display it as a badge of honor. When speaking with others, they speak from ego, pounding their chest and sounding their horn about their journey.

The survivor speaks to themselves in both kind words and negative words. While they give themselves pep talks on how far they have come and how proud they are of themselves, they still tend to talk into the pain and suffering of the past, but with pride. By doing so, they fail to realize they are calling more pain and suffering into the present. This is the issue with the speech of the survivor; by reliving the negative, you are still calling more into existence.

The survivor's speech has transcended the low vibrational fields of force, and they have moved into power. They speak with courage and can inspire others but still carry emotional residue as they have not fully surrendered and still look to control the storyline. They are talking the talk but have not fully committed to walking the walk. They use their words as armor which distorts their speech; it is an attempt to over-manipulate the outcome and not surrender to life's flow. They do not have full faith in their voice and fail to trust the divinity that is behind it.

The Warrior and Their Mouth

The warrior speaks to others in an uplifting, positive manner. They speak from the heart. This does not always mean their words are soft and kind, but necessary to lift those up around them and imbued with faith, trust, and clarity. They focus their words and the conversation on finding the resolution to any dissonance. They look for the light in all their conversations, and do not pass judgement.

Even when obstacles seem insurmountable and the waves of life are crushing down upon them personally and professionally, they find a way to talk through it in a healing and helping manner. They are the holders of wisdom, knowledge, and the keys of understanding and they share their philosophies with all those they encounter and who are receptive, hoping to open the hearts and minds of all that will listen. They listen deeply before speaking and speak only when breath and heart are aligned.

They speak to themselves with words of affirmation. They can be their own coach and be confident when life drops them to their knees and there is no one around to lift them up.

When talking internally, they know when they need words of encouragement and love but also know when they need to be spoken to sternly to fall back into their discipline. They use words that return them to their faith and trust in the divine and allow them to continue their journey to enlightenment. The warrior reminds themselves through their words that they are the light, and they can call in the light even when times are dark. They know their role is to bring the light to the darkness.

The warrior speaks in higher frequencies with words that uplift the mind, body, and soul of all those they encounter, understanding their words are here to repair the world and are a tool for spiritual service. They speak less but speak from divine consciousness to purify the mind, body, and soul of themselves and others.

My journey to Discipline My Mouth

Too often, we speak and we are unconscious of what we are saying. I say this from personal experience. How we speak to ourselves and others is directly correlated to how well we listen to ourselves and others. If we don't listen actively to what the other person is saying, whether it be business or personal, we cannot respond with the correct words.

My insecurities throughout my life have colored my speech. I think this is the case for many people. Many times, I was already crafting a response in my head while the other person was speaking rather than actively listening to the other party. When you listen attentively, you can respond from a place of understanding: understanding their perspective, understanding their situation, and understanding the set and setting of the matter at hand. However, when you are not actively listening, your response can lack compassion and empathy as you may have failed to recognize the emotional setting of the conversation.

I have thought long and hard on why I exhibited this kind of behavior. Many times, it is because I am already in a defensive mindset due to past interaction with this person or due to a similar situation I have been in with others, AKA trauma. Other times, it is because I have a laundry list of things I want to fit in in the conversation. In either case, my speech lacked discipline.

I strive now to listen to the people with attention to their words, body language, emotional cues, and with an awareness of our past interactions that might be coloring the present exchange. Then before I speak, I ask myself three questions: **_1) Is what I am about to say KIND 2) Is what I am about to say TRUTHFUL 3) Is what I am about to say NECESSARY._** My goal is to have all things that I say to others and myself fulfill these criteria. However, I am work in progress, and there are times I do not meet all criteria in my exchanges. Once again, you must give yourself grace to fall out of your discipline. Sometimes, our emotions get the best of us, and we respond from places of anger, anxiety, shame, limiting beliefs, and pain.

Talking at or over people in business or personal situations only leads to more dissonance. Proving a point is not always necessary; rather, resolution and getting all parties back to center when there is dissonance should be the goal. Of course, there are adversarial situations in life where this becomes more difficult, but I still challenge myself and challenge you to be less combative and more understanding.

You also want to make sure when speaking with others that you are speaking to them in a manner that reflects their needs in the conversation. It is very easy to get caught up in what we want, and many times, we show up to conversations pitching our perspective when in fact we should be pitching it from the listeners perspective. This allows you to get all the points across you'd like, but paints the story for the listener. It presents the facts in a set and setting that they understand and makes them feel comfortable and leads the conversation to compromise, understanding, and resolution.

"You are your own worst enemy." There is not a truer phrase for how we talk to ourselves, both out loud and in our heads. I heard this phrase from others a great deal throughout my life. I found it hard to break patterns of self-doubt, limiting beliefs, shame, and fear, and this was clear in the way I spoke to myself and sometimes still speak to myself.

I wish I could say that I never say harmful things to myself, but that wouldn't be honest. What I can say is that when I catch myself speaking in a harmful manner to myself, I pause and correct it with something positive. Reading and listening to motivational and positive messages from gurus and spiritual and religious leaders helps me speak in a more positive way to myself. I have found that if I am filling my ears with negative messaging in the form of music, television, and social media, then this programming colors the way I speak to myself.

We are all guilty of speaking to ourselves in a negative manner and not being kind to ourselves. "I wish I was dead, I am not good enough, I am a failure, it's all my fault, I hate myself, I'm a loser, I really fucked up." If the pronoun was you and you were saying these things to other people, do you think it would help or harm that person or your relationship with them? Clearly, saying these things does not help you manifest your dreams and goals; it brings a negative outlook to any situation. Speaking phrases like these are harmful to your psyche and mental health. So why, then, do we catch ourselves saying them? Why would you want to call in negative energies to your life by saying such harmful things to yourself?

It is helpful to have affirmations written by others and yourself that you speak into each day. My spiritual practice includes mantras form various religious faiths that resonate with me. I speak these mantras to myself in the am when I wake, in the pm when I go to sleep, and throughout the day when I need some uplifting. I wear japa mala beads so I can chant affirmations to myself no matter where I am.

Japa Mala are 108 ritual beads on a necklace; the stone is dependent on preference and the healing needed and being called in. You can use them to chant a mantra or affirmation 108 times.

Why 108? 108 is considered to hold spiritual significance in various faiths and spiritual practice. The number holds astronomical and mathematical significance as well as appears throughout yoga philosophy, scriptures, and cosmology. It is a mystic key number that harmonizes body, mind, and spirit. It's a bridge between the inner self and the cosmos, and repeating a mantra 108 times is believed to attune you to the vibrational frequency of the universe. Mantra repetition is an active way to discipline how we speak to ourselves and purify our mind, body, and soul.

Say something of substance or say nothing at all. We are here for a limited amount of time. We are here to raise the vibration of the world to that of the heavens. Do not waste time on filler conversations. Use your words to learn, to grow, to spread love, to spread knowledge of self, to bring to light to the darkness, and to illuminate the road to enlightenment.

In Summation Self-Discipline – The Burn is the Blessing

Discipline is one's own responsibility. It is a self-accountability on how one chooses to lead their life and what energies one allows in. When we practice discipline, we no longer blame others for the set or setting, our circumstances, our emotions, or our reactions. We no longer live in a victim mentality. Discipline allows one to take control back in their lives rather than let life lead them blindly into low frequency energy spectrums. We become the warrior, and every scene of our life brings a lesson and brings us closer to higher frequencies on our journey to enlightenment.

We practice self-discipline when we cook ourselves in the fires of the mundane world, elevate ourselves to the spiritual world, and transform into a higher version of ourselves. Through this act of self-devotion, we burn off non-supportive behaviors. We lean into our fears and dispel the limiting beliefs they invoke upon us. We forgo momentary pleasures in return for emotional and spiritual growth. Through discipline, we can pass through the obstacles of life and arrive on the other side with greater knowledge of self, but we must be willing to sit in the fires of life. Discipline is the willingness to be both burned and blessed, as both lead to spiritual growth.

Through discipline, we become more discriminatory on what we allow in our lives. Let me clarify this a bit. It teaches us that no matter what shows up in a life, good or bad, from friend, family member or foe, should be viewed as a gift. The question is, do you need to accept that gift? NO. I can politely decline and stay aligned with my inner vibration of love, divine consciousness, and source energy.

Too often, when we lack discipline, we accept all energy, emotions, and messages that come our way. We are reactionary and fail to pause and ask, how is this going to affect my mind, body, and soul? Will it purify me, or will it pollute me? Through our discipline, we can guard against things taken in by the senses that will pollute our energy. We can learn to view them as unattractive and harmful. This concept is not as easy as it sounds. Often, things carrying negative vibrations may look, taste, or sound good. They may even give moments of increased dopamine; they appeal to our desires. One only needs to look to certain food, alcohol, drugs, and music. But like the saying goes about Champagne when overconsumed; perfume going in, poison coming out.

Self-discipline allows one to have a focused and steady spiritual practice even when we are feeling uninspired. We show up for our meditation, prayer, or breathwork session as they become part of our daily routine and are viewed as spiritual anchors rather than chores or inconveniences.

It is self-discipline that allows us to take control of nutritional behavior and view the food we eat as a blessing and nourishment. We no longer look to foods to numb us or to provide us with an emotional escape. Rather, our eating becomes a ritual that gives us clarity, vitality, and energetic flow.

It is through the discipline of our physical fitness routine that we cultivate strength, endurance, and flexibility that aligns our body to our mind and our higher purpose. When we view the body as our sacred temple, we learn that our physical alignment leads to our mental alignment.

We heal ourselves and others when we pause before reacting, when we choose love, empathy, and compassion over anger and hate. When we discipline our senses with respect to our relationship with self and others, we speak with integrity, we listen with compassion, and we think with patience and contemplation. Rather than speak into conflict, we learn to speak into resolution or say nothing at all.

It is through self-discipline that the victim no longer lives in their pain and trauma. Through their practice, they realize that they have survived all the events that once frightened them. They come to the realization that it was the fear of the unknown that was holding them back, but there is nothing to fear as they have been through it and it has only made them stronger. They learn that through their daily practice, they can regain control of their inner power, self-regulate, and shape their reality.

When the survivor leans into their discipline, they learn that they no longer need to wear their past on their sleeve. It is no longer necessary for them to prove to others how strong they are and how much they have been through. They no longer are attached to that story or the happenings of their past. They have let go of the emotional baggage that has held them down and release the limiting beliefs that controlled their mind. They are not their past; rather, their past has molded them into who they are today. Through the consistency of their routine and sitting in the fire of life, they forge themselves into the Warrior.

The warrior lives in the fire because they have realized they are the fire. Their self-discipline allowed them to be one with the fire of life and the physical realm, and through it, they forge themselves into the highest expression of who they can become in this incarnation. They know this is the journey of their souls' correction and there is no destination. There is only opportunity to be better than they were the day before today; to move closer to enlightenment through the attraction of higher frequencies. The warrior understands that self-discipline is the building blocks of being of service to themselves and others, and ultimately of reconvening with divine consciousness.

It is through self-discipline that we can focus on the energy received through our senses, our electricities, and raise our vibration and reach for higher frequencies. We learn to become discriminant of what we let in through the understanding of what effect it has on the purification of our mind, body, and soul. This allows us to stabilize our energy and avoid distractions that could cause energetic crashes.

We develop energetic resilience, which allows one to recover faster from any emotional, physical, spiritual, or mental disturbances that exist in the mundane realm. Disturbances that are detrimental to us on our journey to enlightenment begin to fade away and become insignificant to our story.

Self-discipline is the understanding that the burn is the blessing, and the only way out of the fire is through it. Our ego is no longer the driver of our emotional well-being; rather, we now understand that we are divine consciousness and everything we need for this journey can be found when we turn within. It is through this journey that we attune our vibration to the attractor fields of higher frequencies.

The last few years of my life, self-discipline has taken on new meaning to me. I found myself through my self-discipline, I discovered who I was meant to be in this incarnation, and I committed myself to the mission of Higher Frequencies. Through the various modalities discussed, I was able to gain discipline of my senses. I am no longer shaken by what life throws at me.

I have one guarantee in life: that I can wake up put my feet on floor and step into the day through my discipline. For me, that starts with a regimen of meditation, prayer, physical fitness, and listening or reading of faith-based content. Through this, I become the master of the setting of my day.

Why is this important? Too often, people wake up and turn to the news or their phone, and they lose control of the setting of their mind for the day before they even get out of bed. If you don't take control of the life, life will take control of you. This is accomplished through discipline; there are no shortcuts.

Part 4

The Tools and Practice of Integration

Overview

The following is an offering on tools that I have acquired on my journey to enlightenment. This is not an exhaustive list; there are many other tools that I use and that you may use on your journey. These, however, help me integrate the lessons I have gained in my studies and the downloads I receive through the purification of my mind, body, and soul.

These are the core tools that I found weaved through my studies of various faiths and spiritualities. They are common themes in the teaching of spiritual leaders, religious leaders, great saints, prophets, gurus, and shamans. In some cases, I will reference where the inspiration is drawn from. This is not to give heavier weight to one belief system over another, but rather to show that all roads lead to them same message, the same energy, the same source…Divine Consciousness.

Non-Attachment

Non-attachment is the concept of accepting things when they are meant to be in our lives and allowing them to pass through when they no longer belong. Many times, we hold on to people, places, things, and habits that once brought us joy, but now lead to our pain and suffering. I am not talking about detachment here. Rather, I am speaking of enjoying what shows up in your life and having an awareness and acceptance when it is no longer meant to be there and no longer welcome. It is the awareness that external things we may derive momentary happiness from do not define us and do not own us. Non-attachment is a release of ego, desires, and fear of loss, allowing one to be free from pain and suffering.

Letting Go

Letting go is releasing the inner resistance and suppressed emotions that keep you from reaching higher frequencies. It is through letting go that we allow ourselves to feel our emotions, but we do not hold onto them. It allows us to process the events of the past without judgment of oneself or others. Letting go lets us learn from our past but prevents us from allowing it to define our present or prevent our future. Too often, we allow past events to continue to cause emotional, spiritual, and mental harm. It is through letting go of the story of the past we tell ourselves that we allow ourselves to heal and reach a higher state of consciousness.

Faith and Trust

Faith is the belief that there is a higher power, one that we are part of collectively and one that guides us. G-D, Hashem, Christ

Consciousness, Brahma, Witness Consciousness, many names and many faiths, all leading to divinity: divine consciousness. Trust is the understanding that whatever shows up in your life is neither good nor bad, positive nor negative; rather, it is for you souls' correction. And when we look at it in that light, all things are blessings. I have faith in a higher power and trust that all that shows up in my life was by the design of this higher power to aid and assist me on my journey to enlightenment.

Meditation and Prayer

Meditation is when we turn within and shut off our sense telephones. Meditation is a spiritual practice. It is through meditation that we align our energy with divine consciousness, dissolve our ego, and arrive at the understanding that we are all one. One can and will receive messages through their meditations from a higher power that they can then use to guide them in the physical realm on their journey to enlightenment.

Prayer, often, is faith-based, which does also lead to spirituality. Where meditation we turn inward, prayer we turn outward. Through prayer we ask a higher power to direct us, heal us, aid us, and help us on our journey toward enlightenment. Prayer is aided through the reading of scriptures, the reciting of hymns, and through teachings of religious leaders of past and present.

External Tools

There is one outlier in this part of the book, titled External Tools. I wanted to make sure I included the conversation of entheogens and regenerative medicine, as they have been integral to my journey. Entheogens are psychoactive substances, often derived from plants, fungi, or sometimes synthesized. They are used in spiritual, religious, or shamanic ceremonies to reach higher frequencies. Many can be traced back to the healing practices of many indigenous cultures, but only recently have they taken the stage in the modern world. People are opening their eyes to these sacred substances and their power to purify the mind, body, and soul. Regenerative medicine is becoming a main topic as it relates to healing of the physical body, especially in the conversation of longevity. We will specifically discuss umbilical-cord-derived stem cells or Whartons jelly.

Many of these modalities are still illegal in most of the world and out of reach financially for many. I understand that it is currently a privilege to have access to these medicines. Laws are being passed in states to create roads to access in both sectors. It is my hope to open as many people's eyes and minds as possible to healing with these modalities so the movement for legalization and affordable access can gain further momentum.

Surrender

Let go. Let G-D. Surrender is to live in equanimity. It is the essence of the saying we have heard through this book, you can be in it but not of it: Life. Through surrender, we learn to stop fighting life, and we learn we can be an active participant without adding to our own pain and suffering.

It is the final step when we have learned to practice non-attachment and let go of our ego and the stories we tell ourselves. We must no longer sit in judgment of ourselves and have faith and trust in divinity. When we surrender, we allow ourselves to be in a constant flow state with life and understand what it means to be present, and what is not meant to be will exit our lives with ease and grace. To be all in on life.

The sections are meant to be an introduction to the concepts. There are endless books, talks, podcasts, and other verbal and written mediums that dive deeper and can further your study, guidance, and application. It is through the personalization and application of the following tools that one can have great success in disciplining their senses to purify their mind, body, and soul through their spiritual practice, nutritional behavior, physical fitness routine, and relationship with self and others. Your journey in studying these concepts may start in the below pages, but it is not where it should end.

Section 1 – Non-Attachment

Overview

Non-attachment is the practice of releasing possessions, people, places, habits, and behaviors that no longer serve us. I want to be clear here; I am not saying you shouldn't enjoy these things in your life or derive joy from them. But too often we try to hold on to material items, relationships, and even habits that no longer bring positive energy, that harm us and attract low frequencies into our life. They might have once brought joy, but now they bring pain and suffering through our attachment.

Too often, we become attached to our possessions and hold them as our identity. We open ourselves up to undue suffering when we identify our self-image and identity with things and people. We become incapable of practicing non-attachment. We do all in our power to hold on even when they become a burden due to changes in our economic, business, or personal life.

Practicing non-attachment frees us from suffering. Suffering is caused when we hold onto anything that no longer belongs in our life. When we hold on too long, we can end up suffering emotionally, physically, financially, and/or spiritually. When we recognize that we must exit something from our lives, we release any suffering that would be caused by practicing non-attachment.

We might have outgrown a business or personal relationship, and by keeping the relationship active in our lives, we invite in negative emotions such as inadequacy, jealousy, or anxiety. A once-good habit can even turn into something that causes suffering. For example, I may love to run, but if I break my ankle and it doesn't heal correctly, I need to adjust this behavior as to not cause further suffering. I may find out a favorite food of mine is causing health issues that are detrimental to my well-being. In both instances, I need to practice non-attachment, with the activity and with the food.

Non-attachment invites us to accept things in our life and enjoy their company so long as they do not add to our pain and suffering. It invites us the arrive at the understanding that externalities do not define who we are, and we no longer derive our identity, security, or sense of worth from impermanent aspects of our life, thus allowing us to release anything that no longer brings us to a higher state of being and consciousness, and doing so with the understanding and grace that it no longer belongs in our lives.

When we release what no longer serves us, we create room in our lives for new blessings and experiences to arrive. This always reminds me of the story of the monkey in the three-sided cage. There is a monkey in a three-sided cage. He cannot take his eye off the banana he sees through the bars, but it is just out of his reach. He painfully slams himself into the bars repeatedly, trying to reach the banana. He is fixated on this single banana, but to no avail. He is exhausted and full of anxiety and frustration. He is attached to getting that banana in front of him. However, as mentioned, this cage only had three sides. If the monkey practiced non-attachment and just turned around, he would have seen there were no bars behind him, and within his reach was a whole bundle of bananas. Through non-attachment, we end our suffering and open ourselves up for what is meant for us.

Non-attachment returns us to our inner power. It reminds us that we are an expression of divine consciousness. When we are unattached to the material world, we can turn within and move closer to self-realization. We understand that we are source energy. While we need to be an active player in the physical world, we do not need to attach ourselves to anything in it, especially when that thing brings suffering, pain, or anxiety. We learn that we are enough.

Practicing non-attachment allows us to align with spirit and detach from ego. By doing so we can stop fighting life, return to our breath, live in a flow state, and allow divine timing to align with physical timing. As I have said time and time again, you still need to live in this world. I am not suggesting being detached from this world, but rather to recognize when it is time to let go of anything that brings you pain and suffering. Once again...you can be in it but not of it.

The Victim and Non-Attachment

The victim feels that if they practice non-attachment, they will lose everything. They cannot differentiate between needs and wants. They feel that everything that is in their life is a need, and without it they will cease to exist. The victim is even attached to things that they do not have. They look to others with envy. By becoming attached to things they believe they should have but have yet to obtain, they invite in more suffering, anxiety, and distress. They think, why them and not me?

The victim has a fear-based mentality as they cling to the familiar rather than exploring and accepting the unknown. It is a scarcity mindset. A scarcity mindset is one where one believes they never have enough and will never acquire enough, so they fail to live in the present moment and lack the understanding that they have all they need at the current moment and will not achieve any incremental happiness by acquiring more. They mistake control for safety, and do not realize that safety is an illusion. Life is a gift, and living comes with risks.

The Survivor and Non-Attachment

The survivor feels that they walked through too much fire in life to let go of anything that they acquired or are attached to. They believe these "things" are their badges or patches and wear them with pride on their sleeve. They do not care what it cost them, and even if it begins to lead to pain and suffering, they will not let go. While they may let go of the experiences of getting there, they will remain attached to the outcome, the items, or the emotions.

The survivor may move on from people and habits that cause them to suffer, but they will continue to reference the experiences. This is not practicing non-attachment. Non-attachment says that it happened, and I release it. I don't need to pound my chest to discuss how I am stronger because of it or show others that they didn't have to go through what I did to get here. They fail to realize that all of us are living our own souls' correction, so there is no need to practice comparative analysis. We are all fulfilling our personal karma or tikkun.

Karma is the universal law of cause and effect, or rather, that actions have consequences. In Hinduism and Buddhism, it the philosophical and spiritual principle of the purification of one's soul in this life due to happenings and imprints of your past life. It is not punishment, but rather the balancing of energies as you move through lifetimes on your way to enlightenment and liberation.

Tikkun or Tikkun Olam literally means "repair the world." From a Kabbalistic view, it is the correction and rectification of the soul. It can take many lifetimes to fulfill, but once fulfilled, the soul reconvenes with divine consciousness and is liberated from this physical world.

Karma and Tikkun carry many similarities. They both hold the belief that human actions carry implications past the immediate moment, and energies eventually need to be healed and balanced. The way the soul advances in this lifetime and the next is through challenges that are catalysts for spiritual growth and refinement. This is done through many lifetimes or reincarnations.

Both Karma and Tikkun are faith-based ideologies. We are not being punished when life throws obstacles our way, but rather, all experiences are part of our soul's journey and eventually lead us to enlightenment. It is through the practice of non-attachment that our souls' correction can be fulfilled, ultimately returning us to divine consciousness.

From a materialist standpoint, the survivor won't let go of items that once brought them joy but now bring them sorrow, suffering, and pain. They feel that they "sacrificed" too much already to let go of these things. They will induce more hardships in their life to hold on to things that lower their spiritual acumen and bring them financial distress. They, much like the victim, still feel that these things are part of their identity.

The Warrior and Non-Attachment

The warrior knows that what is meant to be in their life will remain, and what is not meant to be will not. Externalities such as people, places, and things we possess do not define them or make them a better person. The warrior knows they are divine consciousness and are divinely protected. The moment something causes them suffering, they release it and say a blessing, remaining non-attached to things that do not serve them with grace and steadfastness in their practice of discipline. The warrior lives in flow and is present in each moment, understanding it is a gift.

The main goal for the warrior is spiritual and emotional growth. They will not allow possessions to possess them. The warrior lives a life of non-attachment, not detachment. They enjoy all the things that are present in their life at the present moment, but will not sacrifice their mental, emotional, physical, or financial well-being to keep them any moment longer than they are welcome.

Practicing Non-Attachment in Business

One of the areas in life where I find it most important to practice non-attachment is in business. Too often, we lose track of the overall goals of a situation and get to attached to the outcome or destination. We neglect to accept new fact patterns and ignore course corrections that might be necessary to achieve individual and organizational success.

We get so caught up in the "sport of business" that we want to win at all costs. We want the deal to close, we want the paper to be signed, and we want to check the box for the win. Or even worse, we want to "get even" through lawsuits and adversarial proceedings for a wrong that was perpetrated on us. We often put blinders on or fail to see when the relationship or carrying through our mission has become toxic. Whether an entrepreneur or part of a large organization, you must practice non-attachment when it comes to deal flow and deals.

In 2008, I was offered an opportunity to move to Las Vegas and work for Las Vegas Sands, the parent company of the Venetian and Palazzo Hotel Casino and Resort. My position called for me to implement the new strategy of partnerships; however, I ran into a great deal of resistance from individuals and their departments.

An integrated Las Vegas Resort is a self-contained destination that combines luxury accommodations, gaming, dining, entertainment, retail, wellness, and convention spaces into one seamless experience. These resorts typically feature world-class casinos, fine dining by celebrity chefs, immersive shows and nightlife, high-end shopping, spas and wellness centers, and expansive meeting and event venues—all designed to attract both leisure (FIT - Free Independent Traveler) and business travelers. The integration of diverse amenities under one brand and location maximizes convenience, enhances guest engagement, and drives extended stays and higher spending per visitor. It also creates a great opportunity for brands to market to captive consumers through multiple touch points.

Las Vegas Sands developed and once owned the Venetian and Palazzo Resort and Casino. In general, the organizational departments were extremely attached to their goals, their profitability, and the traditional way things were done. At inception, this was the correct strategy; however, as the market and business changed, it neglected to consider cross-departmental efficiencies, new trends, new technology, and collective organizational goals. The individuals and the departments were not very good at practicing non-attachment, which caused their strategies to ignore new ways of doing and collaborating with the organization at large and external partners, also known as strategic partnerships or business development.

First and foremost, working as a silo in a large organization negates that fact that when you pull a lever in one department it has a possible effect on multiple other departments, such as b2b relationships and b2c relationships. The priority in most large organizations is to increase profitability for the owners or shareholders. However, when departments are attached to individual outcomes, they do not act in unison, and they fail to realize that a loss in one department may be an overall gain for the organization.

My view was that through collaboration, we could turn our departments and vendors into partners. The partnerships would open additional sales and marketing channels across the companies collectively and drive greater profits and benefits for all, in turn increasing the overall valuation of all departments and entities.

I started by restructuring the beverage program and working with property marketing to look at new tactics to reach new customers in both the FIT and Tradeshow/Convention Segments. We instituted partnership programs, created the first high-end adults-only luxury pool club, and welcomed the first e-gaming event to the strip.

I courted and contracted one of the largest outdoor spectacular media companies in North America to sell the spectacular signage on the property. Traditionally, this signage was used to advertise the internal offering on property, but there was big money in cross-branding and highlighting partners brands. The company's name I contracted with now adorns many of the digital media platforms on the strip. While spectacular media is now the standard in Las Vegas and digital billboards light up the strip, this was not seen at the time as business opportunity and was frowned upon both externally and internally.

Unlike Times Square, we could connect the brands to the consumer on property and drive experimental engagement. And we had just as many eyeballs. Sales for the brands could occur in multiple areas on property and across multiple consumer segments. We could also offer their consumer giveaways and sweepstakes and cause purchase decisions in retail outlets out of market. It was a win-win for all parties.

Many executives thought it took away from the glamour of the properties. They were attached to the old Vegas and not ready for the new Vegas. In doing so, they ignored new routes to revenue. At the time, our property saw 20 million of the 42 million visitors a year, and as far as I was concerned, we had the eyeballs to make brands and the outlets to sell them.

Over time, I convinced procurement that they were ground zero for opening discussions with potential partners. Due to our buying power and our global construction initiatives, we modified our Request for Proposal (RFP) process. Rather than just looking at deals based on best pricing, we added categories such as property marketing spends, room block buys, convention spends, and omni-channel marketing partnerships. This model is now how many organizations in this sector and others operate.

Looking back on this experience, I might have acted less like as a wrecking ball internally and more as a partner to the other departments and been non-attached to my delivery of the message. That was a key business takeaway. I learned that I didn't need to be the loudest voice in the room, and it was better to find way to create partners internally rather than just point out inefficiencies and correct them by force. It is better to talk into your audience in the language they understand and garner support and buy-in rather than speaking from your point of view. My listening skills lacked discipline, and I was too attached to the story of my ego.

A strategic partnership's main goal is to maximize relationships and assets across all channels. The profits will flow from this, meaning I might pay more for an item in procurement, but that same partner is willing to make up for it by spending two times the appeared loss in another sector of business such as convention, advertising, or room stays. From the perspective of the overall business, it is better to pay for the more expensive item as it is a win for the overall business. We had to break the attachment to the old ways of business to usher in greater prosperity; this is a common theme in business.

If you are in the business world, you must come to the realization that deals are going to turn bad, relationships are going to become toxic, and money will be lost. You must remind yourself that it is just a number, and decide what are you willing to sacrifice for it: your mental health, your physical health, or more money to prove you were "right." None of it is worth it, and you must remain unattached.

I have learned this the hard way time and time again. When you don't practice non-attachment, you can end up harming yourself and the organization further than needed. I can attest to this. When business relationships turn toxic and money is lost, we can fall into the trap of becoming attached to making things right. It may be a friend lying to you and stealing money as discussed earlier, or a deal that seems lucrative hitting regulatory roadblocks, or negotiations breaking down over business or legal obstacles. When this happens, we can end up stealing from ourselves and others. And yes, I am using the word 'steal' to highlight a point.

This is a yogic philosophy, Asteya, or non-stealing, found in the Yamas. We must be careful not to steal from others, ourselves, and nature. When we speak of stealing, we are not merely talking about the act of physically stealing an item, but more specifically stealing time, stealing healing by focusing on the negative, stealing energy by dissipating it on things that no longer serve us or others, and stealing functionality and purpose of relationships and/or interactions.

These are just a few concepts that bleed into the larger philosophy of non-attachment. We must not waste time or energy on things that don't cultivate growth physically, spiritually, or emotionally.

When we become attached to getting even, there comes a point where the negative energy cultivated in the process of "getting even" outweighs the financial or emotional reward, should you ever rebalance the scales. So yes, you are essentially stealing from yourself. You can give yourself a mental health break and let the money go. View the experience as the loss it was and see the benefit gained of the exit of someone or something that should no longer be in your life.

By remaining non-attached, you can divert all that energy that you might have been expanding on being angry to other endeavors that would bring you joy, endeavors that have an emotional and financial payoff in the positive rather than in the negative. Through non-attachment, we can realize when divine consciousness is removing a negative situation from life and move on.

By practicing non-attachment to deals, we allow ourselves to be happier and healthier and move on to the next deal with a clear mind and not allow this past wrong to continue to color our thought process or energy.

Business deals are going to hit roadblocks and breakdown. What once sounded brilliant can become costly and inefficient. As they say, sometimes the juice isn't worth the squeeze. You must recognize when this occurs and practice non-attachment. It can cost more in time, money, and emotional well-being than the amount proposed realized gain.

Non-attachment is a power tool in your business relationships. It allows you to remove emotions from deal flow and take in new facts without the harmful voice of the ego. Business is a battlefield, and you can't sit around and lick your wounds thinking that is going to make them disappear. It's best to move on, practice non-attachment, and turn the loss into a lesson; as the saying goes, "keep it moving."

Practicing Non-Attachment to Things – Materialism

We live in a materialistic world. Many people define themselves by the clothes they wear, the neighborhood they live in, the jewelry they own, and the car they drive. But these possessions can begin to possess us if we are not too careful. It is okay to have nice things and enjoy them, but when they come at the sacrifice of your financial, emotional, and mental health, you are no longer practicing non-attachment.

At one point in my life, I had what many viewed as a sneaker addiction. One might say I was collector, but let's be honest; there is a fine line between addiction and collecting. It never got to the point where I went into debt over it; however, when I shifted my focus from being an executive to being an entrepreneur, I no longer found enjoyment in buying things that didn't further my vision. I still feel that you need to dress for the room, so I didn't give up on my fashion acumen. I just realized I didn't need 600 pairs of sneakers.

This may seem trivial, but at one point, I did feel my sneakers defined me. I was attached to these items and the story that came with them. The reaction I would get when I wore certain pairs, having newspapers do articles on my collection, and the people I spoke to and met because of them all evoked a certain energy and dopamine hit. But I realized it was never the sneakers that made the human connections it was me. I needed to practice non-attachment.

Whether it's your car, the watch you thought you needed for status, the apartment you really can't afford, or the clothes that are out of your budget, one must step back and ask themselves some questions. Are these items furthering my journey toward enlightenment or are they stunting my spiritual growth? Do I own these items or do these items own me?

If they are stunting your spiritual growth in any manner and you still are trying to hold on to them, then you need to assess how well you are applying the maxim of non-attachment. If they are causing you emotional or financial harm, you must let them go. The more we practice non-attachment, the less pain we cause ourselves fighting to maintain things in our life that no longer belong, and the higher our joy and happiness meter rises. Don't let your possessions possess you. It's as simple as that.

Practicing Non-Attachment in Personal Relationships

I think one of the hardest aspects of non-attachment is as it applies is to your relationship with others. I am specifically speaking about friends and family. It is hard to admit when you have outgrown friends, and it is even harder to admit when you have outgrown family. One would hope you never have to turn their back on family. "Blood is thicker than water," but when the relationships with friends or family become toxic or continue to bring on emotional trauma or, even worse, physical trauma, non-attachment needs to be applied.

There is difference between detachment and non-attachment in this case. I am not saying to be emotionless and cut bonds the minute a relationship starts to sour. First and foremost, we must consider if we are making the severity of the situation up in our mind. I am of the opinion that through open communication and clarification, resolution can be achieved in most scenarios with loved ones.

Practicing non-attachment when it comes to relationships is much more delicate as we learn from our loved ones and learning comes with discomfort. Too often, people are coming from a place of judgment rather than seeing other people's points of view, and through putting ourselves in others' shoes we can detach from our story, see their story, and find resolution in the middle. This is where discipline in listening is best applied.

Another factor one must take into consideration is this: is the relationship based in love? Do you love each other unconditionally? Too often, we define love as a give and take, but rather, true love for a friend, a family member, or a partner is the understanding that divinity exists inside of us, and we can share this light and love with each other without the want of reciprocity. All the above considered, if the continued relationship is causing harm and there is no resolution to the situation, then one must apply non-attachment and have that person and their energy exit their life.

I am fortunate that I have never been in a relationship that resulted in physical trauma. But no matter, your age, gender, sex, or ethnicity, no one should ever allow this to occur. There really is no set of reasoning to go through that justifies physical harm. The only option is to practice non-attachment and leave the environment. For many, practicing non-attachment is not a simple on and off switch. If you need help with this maxim, there is no shame; seek it out and lean into it.

<u>Rejection: The Universe and Non-Attachment</u>

There is one last aspect non-attachment that I'd like to discuss here, and that is rejection. Rejection is a way of the universe assisting you in practicing non-attachment. Whether it is with a relationship, a business deal, or the anything else you might feel a sense of rejection with, rejection is the universes' clearing space for even greater opportunity, love, healing, and light.

Too often, we look at rejection as a negative experience. I want to challenge your perspective on rejection. Instead, look at it as a coach helping you practice non-attachment, except that this coach is divine consciousness. When we reframe the story of rejection, we stop chasing people, opportunities, and things that are not meant to be in our lives. We relieve the pressure of having to prove ourselves to others or our ego. Most importantly, we begin to move with the flow of life rather than fight the current.

Non-attachment is not cold or careless—it is the most loving act we can offer ourselves and others. It says: *"I have faith and trust that what is meant for me will stay, and what is not meant for me will go. I do not need to cling to be whole."*

Only when we stop holding on can we rise in love....

Section 2 – Letting Go

Overview

Let's say you broke your arm either by playing your favorite sport, biking, or you just tripped in a freak accident. The arm is set in a cast and begins to heal over the next few weeks. Finally, the day comes, and to your relief, you get the cast removed. And in a few weeks, you're back to full mobility. Would you break your arm on purpose again to remind yourself of the incident? Of course not. Why would you cause yourself physical harm on purpose to remind yourself of an accident that happened in the past? It happened. You can't go back and prevent it from occurring.

Yet we are constantly replaying situations and interactions in our head of the past that do not serve us and cause emotional harm. We rehash conversations with loved ones, business conversations, and other interactions, replaying what we said, how we said it, and what we could have done differently. This only fuels and gives power to emotions of guilt, shame, anxiety, limiting beliefs, and fear of what the future may hold. This is due to our inability to let go of past events and the emotions they conjure up.

I want to be clear here. It is important to learn from your past. As the saying goes, you'll never get where you are going if you don't know where you have come from. But to cause yourself unnecessary emotional pain and suffering does not help improve your own self-image or the relationship that might have been damaged by action or inaction. Furthermore, in most scenarios, we are reliving things in a warped context, colored by other traumas we carry and our own personal biases. The other party might not even be thinking much of the incident you are lamenting over.

Letting go is the concept of releasing thoughts, feelings, beliefs, and emotions that do not serve our highest self. It is the act of practicing non-attachment and understanding that what is meant to be in our lives at a given moment in time will be and what is not meant to be will not be. We let go of emotions that only cause us harm, discomfort, pain, and suffering.

By holding onto negative thoughts about past events, we allow them to birth negative emotions that do not serve our highest selves. Carrying emotions from past events that have exited our lives is useless, as these events no longer exist in real time; they are merely a memory. Therefore, we must LET GO.

Letting go frees us from emotional attachments, which according to all great sages, are the primary cause of suffering. Through the act of letting go we release anger, fear, rage, and anxiety. You give yourself space to feel free, feel happy, and lean into the positivity of your own life. Your focus can then be put towards manifesting what brings you joy rather than what brings you anxiety, pain, and suffering.

You are no longer the victim when you let go and the elements of energy and control return to your life. This allows one to cease being at the mercy of people, places, and things in your environment, and gives you the ability to set the tone for your personal life and business affairs.

One must realize that it's not the thoughts themselves that bring suffering into one's life, but rather the emotions we allow to fester and manifest from these thoughts. By letting go of these negative emotions, you cease to suffer. By letting go of the thought that is causing you to have a negative self-image, you prevent the negative emotion from its ability to return to your psyche. You relinquish its power.

If we do not let go of these emotions, then we tend to handle them in three manners: suppression/repression, expression, and escape. Suppression is the tendency to consciously push feelings down. When we do this unconsciously, it is repression. In both circumstances, we are creating an emotional time bomb within ourselves that can and will manifest at some time or another.

Expression is truly a victim's mentality; we want everyone to know why and how we feel a certain way. It almost always pushes blame on someone else's behavior and actions rather than allowing us to take ownership of the way we are feeling. In turn, it takes away personal control and responsibility over ones' mood and their ability to improve it. It also leads to avoidance of one dealing with ones' feelings by shifting focus to something externally rather than dealing with what is causing us harm internally.

These are all faulty and cause additional harm as we have not let go of the emotions. Rather, we are leaning into coping mechanisms that toxify our health, our mind, our body, and our relationships. Rather than the purification of our mind body and soul, we are adding to internal pollution.

Letting go prevents the mental suffering from leading to physical issues. The concept of mental trauma bringing out physical pains such as inflammation, which is the root cause of many diseases and illnesses, is now something that the medical field is accepting and studying. There are medical treatment protocols, some ancestral, that start with healing the mind to heal the body. By letting go, we allow ourselves to trust the universe and are able lead with love and happiness rather than leading with mistrust, fear, and anxiety.

Letting go allows us to release undue emotional strain and pressure from repressed emotions. When we hold on to negative emotions, we are more prone to experience stress, anxiety, and fear. Ultimately, this can manifest into physical ailments such as muscle weakness, exhaustion, and other injuries that could have been averted by practicing letting go.

Remember, emotions carry frequencies; negative emotions are low frequency, and positive emotions are high frequency. By carrying negative emotions and not letting go, we are preventing ourselves from reaching higher frequencies. This also has a direct impact on the law of attraction, as the frequencies we emit are the frequencies that are attracted. By not letting go of negative emotions, we perpetuate a cycle of negative experiences and negative people showing up in our lives.

Letting go invites us to recognize the emotion or frequency when it arises, but to be discerning when choosing which ones to hold on to or to give strength to. We need to let go of what doesn't serve us and cease any further emotional, spiritual, or mental harm that the past or something out of our control can bring up. That's not to say not to feel feelings from events that happen in your life; rather, we let go of the energy these feelings evoke. We don't want to judge the feeling; we just want to let it exist and exit. By letting go of the negative energy, we do not allow the feelings from happenings to continue to manifest. Negative emotions that we hold on to continue to do harm and put us in a constant zone of suffering.

Spiritually, our goal is to be the witness in life; some call this witness consciousness. In short, it is letting go of the emotions associated with the experiences in your life and practicing non-attachment to those experiences. With non-attachment, I am accepting of anything that is in my life, but I am attached to nothing. I recognize and accept when something no longer is part of my life rather than trying to hold on to something that the energies around me are trying to exit. We no longer are attached to things for our happiness; rather, we are happy for the gift of experiencing life itself.

The Victim and Letting Go

The victim has a very hard time letting go. The past events they feel define who they are, and they want everyone to know and have sympathy for them. It is this woe-is-me attitude that keeps their identity attached to feelings of shame, pain, and resentment. They remain in a low frequency state of mind as they think that holding on to these emotions and memories define them in the past, present, and future. However, it only keeps them living in these low frequency energies. They fail to realize they are the ones giving the negative story line its power.

The Survivor and Letting Go

The survivor is more willing to let go of the past. However, they hold on partially as they would like to make sense of what happened. They practice letting go in parts of their life, but they are still attached to the identity of the "Survivor," meaning they wear the incident as badge. They believe this to be a badge of honor in many circumstances that shows their resolve and endurance.

They are intellectually looking to understand the situation, but at the same time, they are practicing emotional resistance. They are not letting go of what doesn't serve them as they are still lamenting over how they might make sense of its meaning or what they could have done differently. In essence, they do not know how to move on from an incident or event. It is quite ironic, as they know it is in the past but fail to realize no amount of analyzation will change what has already occurred. They do not allow it to rest in the past.

One might say the survivor's actions, when it comes to letting go, are more strategy-based, whereas letting go is a surrender to grace. There is a very big difference between surrendering to emotions and letting it pass through you versus trying to analyze the emotions and their origins to the point where it rehashes low frequency feelings and energies. The difference from the victim is that the survivor wears these feelings with pride and honor for having lived through the situation, making sense of it, and wanting everyone around them to take notice.

The Warrior and Letting Go

The warrior understands that letting go of the past is the only way to set yourself free and open yourself up to the gift of the present and light of the future. Letting go is the understanding that whatever happened to you was part of a divine plan, and that there is no guilt or shame to be felt from your past. Rather, you should have compassion and empathy for yourself, as you have lived through things and you didn't let them break you.

The warrior has made a conscious choice to accept their past as part of their journey toward enlightenment. They understand that without mistakes there would be no room to become a better person. If you had not been wronged by others, you wouldn't know who to surround yourself with as you level up in life. Wrong turns can lead you to the correct destination, and failure is one the best teachers for progression.

The warrior lets go because they know there is no right or wrong when it comes to the road less traveled. There are only lessons, the opportunity to grow and to become the person you are meant to be in this incarnation. The Warrior knows the first step in becoming who you want to be is to know who you don't want to be, and that comes with life lessons through trial, error, discomfort, and failure. Therefore, the Warrior lets go of the past, lets go of emotions that do not serve them, and makes a conscious effort not to repeat actions that are not aligned with their higher self and divine consciousness.

The warrior has internalized that surrender is not weakness—it is their *power*. They no longer suppress emotions, nor do they analyze or justify them. They *witness*, *allow*, and *release*. This opens a universe of positive possibilities and attracts higher frequencies of love, peace, acceptance. Letting go is their daily spiritual practice and their path to liberation. Through letting go, the warrior shifts their perspective from the mundane world to a spiritual perspective and divine consciousness.

My Journey and Letting Go

Letting go has always been an issue for me, as it is for most. I have tendency to emotionally beat myself up over various characters I have played through different points in my life. Often I beat myself up analyzing past situations and the actions I may have taken differently in business and social settings. Letting go is something I have worked on for years and continue to work on today.

Limiting beliefs are an output of not practicing letting go. We all have limiting beliefs. Limiting beliefs are deeply held assumptions or convictions that constrain how we see ourselves, others, and the world. These beliefs—often unconscious—act as mental boundaries that restrict our potential, behaviors, and emotional responses.

From my perspective this was, and sometimes still is, my biggest challenge. When we don't let go of the past, it has a direct impact on business outcomes, business relationships, and personal relationships. This is generally through the creation of limiting beliefs. Limiting beliefs creates roadblocks to opportunities and kill dreams.

A few years back, Mother Ayahuasca once again called me, specifically to work on my limiting beliefs. It just so happened that I was settling a bad business deal that week, but I was having an issue letting go of the preceding events. At the same time, I had made some great strides in my spiritual, physical, and nutritional progress, and was the healthiest I had been in decades.

My intention for the two nights was to work on my limiting beliefs. As I always do, I journaled leading up to ceremony and went in with several questions. However, as we sat down to drink, I couldn't let go of this bad business deal. It was all consuming, so much so that I didn't really feel the effects from a rather large dose of ayahuasca. And when I was asked mid-ceremony if I wanted to drink again, I did so.

As ceremony does, it comes to an end after several hours. While I still felt the effects of the medicine, I followed everyone into the kitchen for some post-ceremony nourishment. I sat down to drink some chamomile tea, and it was lights out for me. I felt the medicine rush to my head. I immediately got up and walked into the garden area only to see the entire landscape fractionalize in front of me. The grass blended into the flowers, the flowers into the trees, and the trees into the night sky. I could see the energy of all these things as one divine green light.

I made it back to my cabin. Fortunately, I had a some Shipibo chants on my phone. The Shipibo tribe are the holders of the medicine, ayahuasca, and their chants have been passed down for thousands of years to aid in ceremony. I got in bed and got right back into ceremony by myself. The chants evoke different energies and serve to assist the medicine in healing one physically, emotionally, and spiritually, both during ceremony and after ceremony.

The next few hours were beautiful but not pleasant. It was one of the few times in ceremony where I saw what one might believe to be negative imagery. I saw rivers of blood filled with Jewish Stars. I came to realize it was a cleansing of generational and personal trauma. The medicine showed me the pain and suffering my lineage had to endure to give me the opportunities that I have today.

The downloads one receives during ceremony sometimes come in codes. It can take hours, days, weeks, months, or even years to fully understand the messaging one receives, and sometimes just as long to integrate. You really need to be gentle with yourself following ceremony.

I opted for a smaller dose the second night, but nonetheless still had a cleansing experience. I always say sitting with ayahuasca is akin to going to a car wash, but in this case, it is your chakras and nadis that are being cleansed. Again, chakras are energy centers in the subtle body that govern physical, emotional, and spiritual functions. Nadis are energy channels through which prana (life force) flows in the subtle body and connects the chakras.

As I was preparing to go into the talk circle the morning after our second ceremony, I wrote myself a note. I had been meaning to give away all my clothing that no longer fit me due to my drastic weight loss. I guess I was unwilling to let go of these physical items because I always felt I would gain the weight back.

I remember the talking stick coming to me, and just as I was about to speak the notes I wrote for that meeting, the download came like a lightning bolt. "I lost all the weight, but I never lost the weight. I lost the physical weight, but I never lost the weight of the shame. And the shame brought on feelings of fear, anxiety, and depression. The shame created limiting beliefs. The shame was a lot heavier than the physical weight ever was or could be."

What shame? The shame of the choices I made with food, drugs, sexual behavior, and how I treated myself physically and emotionally. And of course, how I treated others. I was never violent but at times could be intense and aggressive in business and personal relationships. While I was not this person anymore, I was still carrying the shame, and that was the causal point of my limiting beliefs.

It was time to let go of the shame, the limiting beliefs, and accept the person I was and welcome the person I had become and was becoming with love, empathy and compassion. This is not something that happens overnight but takes time. We need to change how we treat ourselves, and specifically we need to have discipline in how we speak to ourselves and in what we think about ourselves.

Following a breakthrough in ceremony, we are asked to think of something we can do daily for the following two weeks to instill the download in our brain and start to reprogram our psyche and behavior. This is very powerful, and I suggest doing so when modifying behaviors and habits. It is also a good idea to have a person or a group to report it to daily so you have accountability.

My response to this was I was going to say nice things to myself in the mirror in the morning; this was somewhat corny but made me and everyone else smile. Then the room went silent for moment, and our guide looked at me, and asked if she could propose something else. Without hesitation she looked at me and said why don't you get rid of the clothes that no longer fit you. You're not going to need them ever again. She had no knowledge of the note I wrote myself earlier that morning.

It was time to let go....

Physical Benefits of Letting Go	Mental Benefits of Letting Go
1. Reduced Stress Levels 2. Improved Sleep 3. Enhanced Immune Function 4. Lower Blood Pressure 5. Decreased Muscle Tension	1. Increased Emotional Resilience 2. Improved Mental Clarity 3. Enhanced Self-Awareness 4. Better Relationships 5. Increased Happiness and Well-Being

Ways we can Practice Letting Go
1. Mindfulness Meditation 2. Deep Breathing Exercises 3. Identify and Label Emotions 4. Journaling 5. Positive Affirmations 6. Cognitive Restructuring 7. Physical Exercise 8. Seek Support 9. Practice Gratitude 10. Visualize Letting Go 11. Learn from Experiences 12. Set Healthy Boundaries

Section 3 – Faith and Trust

<u>Overview</u>

Spiritual awakening is the realization that we are one with the divine energy of the universe, divine consciousness; the understanding that all faiths and all religions, in their purest form, are about love, moving toward enlightenment, and an interconnectedness of energy. As we are spirits having a human experience.

However, we must remember that we need to live and operate here in the 3D. It is where the work happens for your souls' correction and where you "SHOW UP." It is where we heal ourselves, our energy, and help heal those you meet in both your business and personal life. We are all on a mission to raise the mundane world, the physical world, to the spiritual world. In other words: be a part of the global spiritual awakening.

How does one define the pillars of spiritual awakening, especially when it is not something that can necessarily be taken in by our physical senses? Let us examine the concepts of faith and trust as these pillars. Faith is the realization that there is a higher power, a higher energy that is guiding and connecting all things in the physical form. Some may call this energy God, Brahma, Hashem, Source, Witness Consciousness, Christ Consciousness, or Divine Consciousness. It is not the physical manifestation of a being but rather the concept of a divine energy or light that is present in all things. At a higher level of consciousness, it is the realization that we are all manifestations and expressions of this divine energy.

Trust is bit more complicated. You see, we are all born into different experiences. The obstacles we face as individuals vary greatly based on our socioeconomic situations, the family we were born into, our environment, and physical aspects of the human condition such as medical and health challenges. This is where trust comes into play. Trust in the divine; trust in divine consciousness. Trust is the realization, self-realization, that no matter what is happening in life, it is for our greatest good and for our greatest enlightenment. What is happening around us and to us is meant to aid in our journey to enlightenment, so we may, our soul may, eventually reconvene with the divine.

Faith is the understanding that there is a greater energy that is guiding us. Trust is the understanding there is no good or bad that happens to us, but rather all things that are transpiring in one's life are guided by the divine, and thus allowing one to work through their soul's correction toward enlightenment. It is through trust that we can stop fighting life. Trust allows one to live in equanimity. Through trust we can move into witness consciousness and lean into the love and beauty that surrounds us.

Trust is the process of letting go and practicing non-attachment. It involves letting go of excessive worry, energies, and emotions that do not serve us and anxiety they promote. We trust that things will work out in the end. We trust that all situations the divine puts us in are for our greatest soul's correction. And through this trust, we always walk away with a lesson.

This doesn't mean to sit back and not be an active participant in life; you must show up and be a participant in all situations, but you cannot allow the stories in your head to prevent you from moving forward, no matter the circumstances one is presented with. Too often, we get paralysis by analysis, but if we trust in the divine, we can act no matter what scenario our mindstuff is creating, and we can purify our mind, body, and soul.

Trust is faith in action, knowing things will unfold as they are meant to be, even in the face of uncertainty or challenges. It is through faith and trust that our spiritual awakening is allowed to take shape, and we are allowed to "level up" into a greater spiritual, physical, emotional, and mental being. We are able work through the energies that no longer serve us and further align with the energies that allow us to be the best version of ourselves in this incarnation.

We can accomplish this through disciplining our senses; by sitting in the fire of life and allowing it to burn off what doesn't serve our spirit, our soul, and eventually becoming the fire itself. When you can delay momentary gratification through discipline, you are rewarded with spiritual growth and enlightenment. This process allows us to purify our mind, body, and soul.

Too often, we look externally for momentary dopamine hits, forgetting that we are connected to the divine and have access to unlimited happiness, love, and energy. All we must do is turn within, cultivate that energy, and share it with others without wanting any form of reciprocation.

When I think of faith and trust in a higher power, I think of discipline in speaking and thinking, specifically how we speak to ourselves and others. Whether we are speaking out loud or when we are having a conversation with self, we are calling things into existence. The power of the spoken word is a concept that can be found in most faiths and spirituality.

You may also know it by its actions such as prayer and meditation. Too often, we lack discipline and think because we aren't praying or meditating that we are not calling things into being through our speech and thought patterns. The reality is that anytime we are speaking or thinking we are having a discussion with the universe. You are attracting energies through your speech and thought, and whether they are negative or positive has much to do with outlook on your situation. But one thing is for certain; the universe is listening.

The Victim, The Survivor, The Warrior, and Faith and Trust

Let's look at this another way. How would the victim, the survivor, and the warrior speak with respect to faith and trust in the Divine? I believe it would go something like this.

1. Victim
    a. Faith: How can there be a God when this is happening to me?
    b. Trust: How can I trust that everything that is happening is for my greatest soul's corrections, when I don't know if there is a God and I am not sure I have a soul?
2. Survivor
    a. Faith: I have faith there is higher power, but I also believe there are negative forces at play that want to stunt my growth and cause harm to my psyche.

    b. Trust: I want to trust that everything is for my greatest good, but I also live in the real world and expect "negative" things to happen to me.

3. Warrior
    a. Faith: All things that show up in my life come from the one divine source that we all emulate from and one day will return too.
    b. Trust: I trust that anything that enters my life is for my greatest soul's correction and is being directed by divine consciousness. I trust I am divinely protected no matter the circumstances, happenings, or outcomes. It was written.

The victim lacks faith and trust. They are unable to surrender at all. The survivor understands faith and trust. While they believe in divine consciousness and its power in manifesting in their lives, they still believe they can manipulate the playing field of life. They are not ready to surrender to divinity, as they feel divinity still owes them something.

Now take this a step further and think about all the times you speak negatively to yourself and to others. Imagine each time you do so, you call into existence that negative energy, and that negative energy creates increasingly more negative occurrences and experiences. This is the victim and survivor's mindset. The victim harps on the negative only to be confronted with more of the same "disasters in life." The victim lives in the shadows. The survivor talks about their trauma molding them into who they are but is always waiting for the next weight to drop. The survivor finds warmth and comfort in the darkness.

The warrior practices full faith and trust in the divine. They remain in equanimity no matter the set and setting. While they are active participants in life, they have an absolute awareness that there is a higher power guiding them on their journey to enlightenment. They do not fight the waves of the ocean of life; they ride them.

The warrior took the lessons from the experiences and has complete faith and trust in the divine. They understand that no matter what has occurred to them in the past or might be on the road ahead, the road less traveled is for their greatest in enlightenment. The warrior arrives ready to receive the love and light of all experiences, they see no negative or positive, they only see growth and love.

My Journey Through Faith and Trust

I was always proud to be Jewish; we celebrated all the major holidays in my household. But I never really embraced what it meant to be Jewish. It was more about going through the motions, understanding where our people came from, and that many of my family members were murdered during the Holocaust. I didn't go to Hebrew school but rather did an "amended" set of lessons for my Bar Mitzvah.

In my household, we were more focused on our spirituality. My parents instilled in us the understanding that all faith and all religions, if practiced with love, lead you to the same place, God or Divinity. As previously mentioned, my parents, while both Jewish, met at Christmas Mass. Rather than going to temple weekly, they would make sure we meditated daily.

In my mid-thirties, I started to have a new curiosity about what it meant to be Jewish, or Judaism not as just a religion but as one of many paths to spirituality and enlightenment. I tried to go to various temples, but felt that the services were more operational than spiritual.

One day, I walked to my bookshelf and noticed a book I had never seen and didn't know where it came from: *Garden of Emuna* by Rabbi Shalom Arush. It was a collection of stories on Emuna, which in Judaism translates to Faith. Faith in a higher power. It resonated so greatly with me that I named the regenerative medicine business I was working on at the time Emuna Wellness.

Emuna goes beyond intellectual belief and is the embodiment that there is a higher power that is guiding our soul's correction. It asks us to have faith in this higher power and an understanding that nothing is random in our life, and even struggles are opportunities to learn to refine our character, heal our karma, elevate our consciousness, and love ourselves and others to a greater level.

Emuna teaches us to live with equanimity even when life might seem chaotic, aiding in the purification of our mind, body, and soul. Through our faith we align with higher frequencies, dissolving fear, doubt, and despair while leaning into trust, surrender, and higher consciousness on our journey to enlightenment.

And the journey continued as I was walking to a meeting in Malibu and a gentleman on a bike road up to me and asked about my shirt, Higher Frequencies. We discussed the ethos of the brand, and he said it sounded like his brand, which was about Divine Providence. Turned out his brand was Judaism, and he was the Rabbi for the Chabad of Malibu. He invited me to Shabbat dinner and game me copy of the Torah with spiritual commentary by Rishi. Hashem was allowing me to discover my Judaism in a mystic and spiritual light.

About two years later, I decided to take a trip on my birthday to Costa Rica. On the day of my birthday, I found myself at a hot spring in Arenal which I was not meant to be at. As I was exploring, I stumbled upon a family, and the husband immediately took notice of my Jewish Star tattoo. I immediately realized he was a Chabad Rabbi. He was on vacation with his family from Orlando. What are the chances of this encounter? I said I wasn't supposed to be there, and his response was "You absolutely are, and have you prayed today?" He immediately went to his car and got a tefillin, and we prayed together as the sun set over Arenal, an active volcano in Costa Rica. The burn is the blessing.

Tefillin are scared instruments in the Jewish religion. The instruments themselves are made of two boxes, each with leather straps. Within the boxes there are pieces of parchment paper that contain the Torah passages that command this mitzvah essentially stating God's unity and love, the Shema Prayer, and our responsibility to love G-D.

One wrap and box is placed around the arm and the other around the head. A prayer is said prior to each leather strap being fastened. The significance of this daily practice is tying oneself to G-D's unity, binding the ego, and liberating the soul from physical enslavement. Through this practice we draw down the divine light. We unite mind, body, and soul and connect to divine consciousness.

Upon my return to Los Angeles, the rabbi I met in Costa Rica suggested I meet with his friend who was the Chabad Rabbi in Hollywood, a young French Jew who was as eager to learn from my spirituality as I was from his path. He suggested I come with him to buy a tefillin so I could add the daily Jewish Ritual to my spiritual practices. He suggested I read the book Gates of Trust. I had asked G-D to connect me to the spirituality contained in my Judaism, and it was occurring in real time. So began my studies of the concept in trust in the divine.

Gates of Trust, Sha'ar HaBitachon, was written by Rabbeinu Bachya Ibn Paquda in the 11th Century. It is a mystical discussion on the inner discipline of Trust, placing absolute trust in divine consciousness; G-D, Hashem. I feel this applicable to whatever name you want to call divine consciousness dependent on your faith and spirituality. Whether you use the name Hashem, Christ Consciousness, Brahma, divine consciousness, or any other name, they are all reflections of one source energy.

Divinity was talking to me through the universe as I read Gates of Trust. Bitachon (Trust) is the concept that we trust in all Hashem/G-D brings into our life as it is for our greatest soul correction. There is no positive or negative: only personal spiritual development. Between the businesses and personal dealings, I had felt like the fire of life was all consuming. After reading this book and studying the concept contained within, I realized the fire was healing, cleansing, and preparing me for my greatest awakening and enlightenment. I realized that I was the fire.

In the Jewish religion, we take twenty-four hours of rest on the sabbath. It is a time to disconnect from the world and to connect to loved ones and divinity. I hadn't been observant of this ritual, but I began understanding its importance. Being that I was living in LA and far from blood family, I started to host non-denominational Shabbat dinners. I wanted to create a set and setting of friends and family where we could celebrate life and lean into each other for support during both calm and turbulent times. I was reconnecting to my faith in Judaism, beginning my studies of Kriya Yoga, and participating in plant medicine ceremonies. Through these dinners I was able to reconnect with friends, family, and myself. There was dialogue on life, love, and everyday struggles. We listened and shared with compassion rather than judgment, and through this opened each other up to the healing of divine consciousness.

It doesn't matter your faith, so long as you have faith and do not judge your brothers and sisters, Trust the process and reawaken the divine light in your heart through the pure calm light that exists in us all. It is up to us to take the power back from those that want us divided. It is up to us to realize that we must work toward resolution and understanding. That is Higher Frequencies, the understanding that all roads to lead to divinity. And through conversation, empathy, and compassion, we can become enlightened to the common threads of energy that connect us all.

Trust in G-D means relying on source for all needs, without fear of people, fortune, or circumstances. I have mentioned it time and time again in this book; all things that show of up in my life are for my greatest good. I have faith that there is a higher power and I trust that this higher power governs over every detail on my life, and that all divine consciousness brings into my life is to help, heal, purify, and enlighten my soul.

Cultivating trust bridges the human and the divine. Through this trust, we learn to live free from anxiety and worry and learn to cultivate peace and joy regardless of external conditions. Through trust, we learn to live with serenity, faith, and purpose, and are open to receive the love and prosperity the universe is willing to offer.

Our spiritual practice (meditation and prayer), nutritional habits, and physical fitness routine are all things that guide us in this process, assist us in being our best selves, and align us with our and the universe's HIGHEST FREQUENCIES.

Taking time to celebrate our faith and trust in the divine is extremely powerful. When we take moments to reflect on our blessings and share our gratefulness with the ones we love, we invite more light and love into our lives. It is important not only to do this in your daily spiritual practice but also with others.

<u>Key Elements of Spiritual Awakening, Faith, and Trust</u>

Key elements of a spiritual awakening include self-discovery, expanded consciousness, shift in priorities, emotional release, increased empathy and compassion, seeking meaning and purpose, altered perception of time, and connection with something greater, AKA the Divine.

Key elements of faith include belief in the divine, trust in the divines promises or downloads we receive through meditation and prayer, devotion and loyalty to a higher power, commitment to spiritual practice, and acceptance of the concept of divine providence.

Key elements of trust include trust in a higher power, reliance on divine providence, letting go of excessive worry, having faith in positive outcomes, applying the practice in your daily life, and having a spiritual practice.

A Prayer for Faith and Trust....

My Mind is filled with Light.

My Body is filled with Light.

My Heart is filled with Light.

My Soul is one with Divine Light.

Lead us from darkness to light…

Lead us from ignorance to wisdom…

Lead us from hate to love…

Lead us from restlessness to bliss…

Lead us from harming each other to helping each other…

Purify our mind, body, and souls so we may reach our highest frequencies…Journey to Enlightenment.

Section 4 – Meditation and Prayer

Overview

Many people often use the terms meditation and prayer as synonyms; however, in my opinion this is the not the case. Both modalities are used to achieve higher consciousness and to connect to higher frequencies, but they do so in different manners. One is focused on faith and reverence for a higher being, and the other is focused on turning inward to connect with the energy of the universe and all it encompasses. When one prays, they pray to their deity or a higher power. When one meditates, they understand that there is no separation, and they are one with divine consciousness. Both modalities bring healing, and both are necessary parts of ones' spiritual practice.

Prayer is often associated with faith-based religions. Through prayer, one seeks connection with God, a bond expressed in different modalities and methods depending on the tradition one follows. In prayer, we call upon the divine's healing power—the source of all energy.

Methods of prayer may be articulated in scriptures, passed down through ancestral lineage, and through the writings of prophets, gurus, shamans, and various other medicine workers. Prayer is the yearning to call out and connect to a higher power, and to show that higher power reverence and ask for healing. Through prayer, we align with our faith and ask for the purification of our mind, body, and soul.

Generally, when one prays, they are asking for a certain aspect of life to be fulfilled or for certain healing to take place in the physical realm we live in. They are turning their attention to a higher power and asking that higher power to provide healing, guidance, and signs, and to illuminate the most righteous path for themselves, their loved ones, and human beings across the Earth. One might say it is almost a tribal experience, as there are a set of precepts that are to be followed based on a particular book of faith or ancestral teachings. It is through prayer that we find connection to something greater than the individual.

Meditation is the silencing of the mind and disconnecting its' connection to the five sense telephones. Through meditation, one strengthens their soul's connection to a higher state of consciousness, divine consciousness. Rather than asking a higher being for something to be delivered upon the individual, the individual is connecting to the universe and pure consciousness. Through meditation, we can silence our mind and understand that all things are energy, and all things are interconnected. We can attune ourselves to higher frequencies.

Meditation breaks down the illusion or delusion of what is created by our five senses. It reminds us that through a clear mind, we can live a harmonious life filled with love and positivity. It is a way to silence the noise of everyday life and breakthrough to our higher being. But we are not asking for anything in return, as we do in prayer; rather, we are looking to empty the space the noise the modern world occupies in our mind, the noise that leads to depression, fear, and anxiety, the noise that keeps us rooted in the mundane world and disconnects us from the spiritual world and our souls' purpose.

Through meditation, we look to disconnect and stop answering our sense telephones that are constantly ringing us with information, some useful and some useless, some helpful and some harmful. When we meditate, we allow our being to be in perfect flow with the universe. We find equanimity in our daily lives.

The universe begins to provide the answers to the questions we may have in our daily lives through the silence we arrive at in our meditation. It is also a great way to release stress and anxiety as it is a break from the noise of everyday life. Through meditation, we realize we are a manifestation of divine consciousness.

There are various forms of mediation and within those forms various teachings.

- **Guided Meditation** involves a voice leading the practitioner into a relaxed state of consciousness, often through storytelling or descriptive cues designed to clear the mind.
- **Sound Meditation** has become increasingly popular. It uses instruments such as singing bowls, gongs, or drums to help the practitioner access higher frequencies. The vibrations assist in clearing mental clutter and external noise.
- **Mantra Meditation** uses repeated words or phrases—chanted aloud or silently. The vibrations of these mantras invite higher frequencies and allow the practitioner to block out distractions from daily life.
- **Silent Meditation** is practiced by closing the eyes and attuning solely to the sound of the universe, known as *AUM*. Considered the primordial vibration, AUM is regarded as the highest frequency.
- **Breathwork Meditation** employs intentional breathing practices to regulate the flow of energy throughout the body. These techniques align the practitioner with higher frequencies and foster deeper connection to the soul beyond the physical conditions of daily life.

- **Yoga**, which means "to yoke," represents the union of mind, body, and spirit. While often associated with physical postures, yoga is also a meditative practice that aligns one's energy. Some forms are physical, while others are primarily mental or emotional, each serving as a path toward higher awareness.

There is no single "right" way to meditate—different practices may resonate with different people. What remains constant, however, is the goal: to move closer to bliss and enlightenment. A key aspect of this journey is learning to be free from desire. Desire is often the root of pain and suffering, and meditation helps us release its grip.

As one wise saying teaches: *"Let your desires hang loosely on your soul. The more lightly we hold them, the less we suffer. When desire is removed, pain and suffering dissolve. Desire nothing, and know that you already have everything."*

Meditate on that.

Prior to moving forward and discussing the archetypal viewpoints on prayer and meditation, it is important to state that any form of prayer and meditation is a step in the right direction. One should never be discouraged about where they are on their journey to enlightenment. You can always have an awareness of where you are at and where you would prefer to be, but taking an active stance to begin the journey of your prayer and meditation practice is an accomplishment.

The Victim and Meditation and Prayer

Those with a victim mindset feel their prayers are never answered. There is a desperation inherent in their prayers. This stems from the expectations they place on how their prayers should be answered, in the exact manner they are requested. Those in a victim mentality view prayer as bargaining with the divine, and if their prayers aren't fulfilled as requested, they feel they have not been answered. As they say, "god works in mysterious ways." It is best to not have expectation when we prayer. The victim doesn't know how to let go and let God.

When it comes to their meditation practice, the victim has a hard time turning off their senses and turning within. Meditation can be frustrating as the victim cannot stop the constant restlessness of their mind. It is their pain and suffering that defines them and their mind and ego that keeps the energies of fear, anger, and despair pulsating. If they were to have success in meditation, they feel they would cease to exist as their pain wouldn't be seen by others.

The Survivor and Meditation and Prayer

The survivor approaches prayer with expectations as they feel they are owed an answer to them. In their view they have fought the battle, have the scars, survived the trauma, and are due to have their prayers answered. They see prayer as divine consciousness balancing the scales of justice and life, and are often let down by the outcome but still pray in hopes of change.

There are constant distractions when the survivor tries to meditate. The distraction is both internal and external. When they turn within, they meditate on their accomplishments, the road and struggle it took to get to the present moment in time. While they find healing through this, it is based on pride, and they never arrive at silence. Since they never arrive at silence, they never truly shut off their sense telephone. They cannot fully live in equanimity.

Their connection to divinity is filled with the static noise of the badges of their trials, tribulations, and trauma. They believe that it is through their suffering they unite with divine consciousness. However, through their prayer and meditation practice, they begin to ground, calm their nervous system, and rebuild their faith, confidence, and trust in the divine.

The Warrior and Meditation and Prayer

I am Blessed, I am Grateful, I am Appreciative; I Love Myself; I Love Others, I Love All. I Love; My Love Unifies and Empowers...." This is the prayer of the of the warrior. The warrior welcomes divinities' answers to their prayers in any manner they arrive, for the warrior knows that the set and setting of the answer to their prayers is ultimately best left to divine consciousness. It is through their prayer practice that the warrior learns to "Let Go Let God." Divinity will answer their prayers in a manner that is for their greatest lesson, healing, and soul's corrections, and the answers will illuminate the road on their journey to enlightenment.

It is through meditation the warrior understands there is no separation between their soul and divine consciousness. The physical body keeps them rooted in the mundane world, but their soul remains divinely connected to source. They are one with source energy. They view their meditation practice as sacred. It is time for them to connect with divine consciousness and temporarily disconnect from the physical world. During their meditation, the warrior gives the spirit a break from having a human experience. They disconnect from the physical and mundane world.

The warrior finds healing and rest in the silence and becomes one with the universe. To the warrior, their practice is a training in spiritual mastery. They approach it in a consistent manner with purpose and discipline. It aids in sharpening their awareness, dissolving their ego, and aligning them with higher frequencies. Through their practice, they return to their body balanced and ready to purify the mind, body and soul. The warrior shares their practice and healing with others without the want of reciprocity. They live in equanimity.

My Meditation and Prayer

Meditation and prayer are part of my daily purification process. I am blessed, grateful, and appreciative that this has been the case since before I was able to walk. My day begins and ends with a combination of both meditation and prayer. It creates a set and setting for my mind as it navigates the waters of life and its lessons. When I find myself out of balance, I take a moment to meditate or pray. Through my practice, I am reminded that divine consciousness is always listening and is omnipresent.

On my journey, I have studied with Rabbis, Gurus, Monks, Shamans, and other enlightened souls. All the great faiths put importance on both meditation and prayer as a daily practice. While we must be active participants in the world we live in, we must also make time daily to align our energies with what can't be observed through our sense telephones. It is through prayer and meditation that we allow ourselves to vibrate higher and reach higher frequencies.

I find it helpful to set time aside when I wake up and when I go to sleep. In the am I wrap tefillin, chant several mantras from my Hindu and Buddhist studies, meditate silently, and read scriptures from various faiths. In the pm I do not get into bed without repeating a series of mantras from various faiths.

I also treat my yoga practice and some of my physical workouts such as biking and running as moving meditations. It is through these activities that I reconvene with the divine through my breath. When I find the noise of my business and personal life to become overwhelming and noisy, I step aside and meditate for ten to fifteen minutes.

Group meditation and prayer can have profound effect on one's personal spiritual practice and journey. While it is important to have your personal practice, you must also make time to practice with others as the combined focus and energy can open doorways of spiritually that one might not have access to alone. This is not limited to places of worship, although they are a good starting point. Nature is another great place to be with a group to meditate and pray.

Lake Shrine became such a refuge for me following the pandemic. When I started visiting Lake Shrine Self Realization Center for Sunday services, I was reminded of the importance of being in spiritual dwelling with others. The higher frequencies cultivated in the Temple during these meditations and faith talks brought me levels of calm, clarity, and enlightenment that helped me in ways that cannot be fully expressed in words.

There is a saying in yoga: it is a practice not a perfect. This is true of meditation and prayer as well. These are not choirs; they are aids on your journey to enlightenment, and in being so, should make your energy feel lighter not heavier. It is okay to try different modalities until you find ones that harmonize you and aids in the purification of your mind, body, and soul. Many masters have said it can and will take a lifetime, or multiple lifetimes, to become an expert in your meditation and prayer practices. Your practice is not something you should ever get discouraged about; the more we lean in, the more light we receive, and the more healing enters our life.

Chants, mantras, books of faith, and ancestral teachings are all guides on your journey to enlightenment. All of these are aids in your prayer and meditation practice. All roads lead back to the same realization; through both prayer and meditation we feel the omnipresence of divinity and come to the realization that there is no separation. We are one with source energy and we further our connection through our practice. When we realize all things are energy, we can align our vibration with higher frequencies. Everything we want and need will arrive with ease, grace, and love, so long as our prayers and meditation come from a place of love.

Section 5 – External Tools

Entheogens: To Purify the Mind and Soul

Overview

Entheogens are substances that, when used with intention, aid one in reaching heightened states of consciousness and connecting to divine consciousness. They are often used in medical, spiritual, religious, or shamanic settings. They can be helpful in healing trauma, PTSD, anxiety, and other emotional obstacles that impede one's journey to enlightenment. In some cases, they have medical benefits such as creating neuroplasticity. While it is one's goal to have the ability to return to breath and elevate their consciousness through meditation and prayer, entheogens can be a beneficial aid in clearing energy blockages and aiding and accelerating healing in the process of purifying the mind, body, and soul.

Most of these medicines are still illegal or highly regulated in the United States and globally. One must do their own research when they consider partaking in any of the below healing modalities. My goal here is to give an overview of what is available, what it may assist with, and to open the discussion to those who it may help.

It is my belief that legal access should be explored in three pillars, and in some cases, it is already being explored in these manners at the state and federal level. Pillar one would be in conjunction with the pharmaceutical industry. We need to rethink healthcare in this country and move from sick care to a more holistic approach.

Many of these medicines carry substances that can be isolated, removing the psychedelic experience, while still aiding in the healing and treatment of various diseases and ailments. And in some cases, the participant may need clinical guidance/supervision or a prescription with certain entheogens such as MDMA, Ibogaine, and LSD.

Pillar Two would be in the consumer product goods category (CPG). We have already seen this with cannabis, and we now need to think about psilocybin, "magic mushrooms." While I can understand wanting certain entheogens to go the route of the pharmaceutical industry, I do not understand this when it comes to psilocybin, a fungus, especially when we are discussing its use as a supplement or over the counter aid, as a supplement used in microdoses to aid in anxiety, depression, and other emotional hurdles.

There are many things on the market that are addictive, and can cause death and even impairment past the point of being in control. We allow these items to be bought and sold and assign personal reasonability. In some cases, we set up laws to prevent people from doing things like operating a vehicle or heavy machinery under the influence. The medical benefits with psilocybin are too great to ignore and too great to limit access. Through a regulated CPG market, we can control efficacy, messaging, and purity. Currently, there are products on the traditional (illegal) market that ignore all of these, and we are putting people in need of help at risk.

Pillar Three would be in a ceremonial setting. Many of these medicines are considered ancestral medicines. They are from the earth, and their lineage traces back to various tribes and ethnicities. When partaking, one must be aware of the legalities surrounding these substances. They must use their own judgment on the risk of proceeding from a legal and health prospective. One must also make sure they are proceeding with the correct respect for the lineage that the medicine traces back to. Discussions like indigenous rights, indigenous reciprocity, and manners in with the way the medicine is being procured and harvested all must be addressed and explored.

When I work with these medicines, I do so in traditional lineage settings. However, I also understand that these medicines have tremendous healing power and can have a dramatic impact on the global mental health epidemic, and there needs to be greater access. My suggestion for ceremony work would be to set forth some form of traceability for the procurement of the medicine and some sort of self-regulating body similar to the Registered Yoga Teacher RYT for yoga. This would ensure that the medicine was procured ethically and under the correct conditions, and that those officiating ceremonies were properly trained with respect to risks and understand the traditions of the ancestral culture that should be honored in the ceremonial work.

The most important part of the process and use of these medicines is setting one's intentions prior to ceremony and their willingness to do the work and integrate after the ceremony or psychedelic experience. Guided and accredited assistance such as therapists, religious leaders, spiritual leaders, coaches, and other behavioral development professionals can be a great benefit.

However, one must make sure they are aligned with those they work with, they have the proper references, and they too are coming from a healthy emotional mindset. These professionals can help you set the proper intentions, decode the downloads, and give you guidelines to assist in the integration in the weeks and months thereafter. For a myriad of physical and emotional reasons, one must properly vet and align with whomever is guiding them through the healing.

Prior to partaking in these medicines, it is important to set clear intentions. These intentions can be based on healing past trauma, general development work or other emotional obstacles you are currently facing on your journey to enlightenment. The more definition you can set to your intentions going into the experiences, the greater the benefit you receive coming out. With one caveat, you may have clear set intentions, but what you uncover in ceremony may only be a door to larger work that must be done. Ultimately, the medicine will guide you so long as you are open to receive the messages.

Integration may also be supported by prayer groups, meditation groups, community centers, fitness classes, and journaling. Everyone needs to find the best way to integrate after one of these experiences. In some cases, one experiences ego death, and in other cases, one realizes they no longer are fond of the avatar they have been playing, and maybe that is one in the same thing. You may have to disassociate from people, places, habits, and things that no longer serve you, which can be isolating and lonely. Integration and the willingness to do so is the most important step in the process of healing and using this medicine as a catalyst to do so. You must be willing to do the actual work.

The Medicines

Ayahuasca

Ayahuasca, vine of the soul, is a brewed tea that has been used for centuries by indigenous cultures in Peru, Brazil, Ecuador, and Colombia. Traditionally, it is administered by shamans to heal illness, cleanse energy, and connect to spirit realms. The active ingredient is DMT, the spirit molecule which is also found in Psychotria viridis (chacruna leaf). This leaf is brewed and combined with Banisteriopsis Caapi (the vine) which carries the necessary alkaloids that enable DMT to become active. There may be other herbs added to the brew, but these are the primary ingredients for Ayahuasca.

Mother Ayahuasca, as she is the grandmother of all the teaching and healing plants, is viewed as a teacher or guide that opens us up to higher frequencies. Icaros and other sacred songs are chanted during the ceremony to call forth different healing spirits, guide visions, cleanse energy, and assist with any discomfort. Aside from visions, one can also experience a physical purging in the form of vomiting, crying, sweating, and other bodily excretions. Many feel this is an important part of ceremony as the purge is negative energy being released. These ceremonies can last anywhere from four to twelve hours, depending on the strength of the tea and the amount of times the individual drinks the tea over the course of the night.

There are both spiritual and scientific benefits to ayahuasca. The indigenous have been using these plants as guides for healing and spiritual evolution for millennia. People, me included, can attest to having visionary experiences that have changed who we are and their life for the better, helping to resolve trauma and other forms of suffering that had stunted our emotional and spiritual growth, releasing us from limiting beliefs. From a scientific perspective, we are just getting started, but studies are now under way to analyze how DMT leads to altered states of consciousness, has a profound effect on neuroplasticity, and can possibly help with neurodegenerative diseases.

5-MeO-DMT (Bufo Alvarius – The Toad)

5-MeO-DMT, Bufo, is procured from "the poison" contained in the defense secretions of the Bufo Alavirus Toad (the Toad). The Toad is found in Northern Mexico and the Southwestern U.S. Its secretion is a powerful, naturally-occurring psychedelic. There is an active debate on when exactly this medicine began to be used in ceremonial work by the indigenous culture in Mexico. For this reason, I am going to refrain from calling it an ancestral medicine.

Bufo differs from ayahuasca in a few ways. First, it is not a tea. The secretion from the toad is crystallized and smoked. The onset is almost immediate, whereas ayahuasca can take anywhere from forty-five to ninety minutes to feel the effects. Bufo is an extremely intense experience that lasts about fourteen to fory-five minutes. During this time, many say they have a sense of ego death, and that they are shot through space into pure light. They feel their spirit leave their body, and they reunite with divine consciousness.

When you arrive back from your altered state, the world and your surroundings look very different; there is a glow and energy you see in all things that can only be fully understood once you have been through the experience. These experiences are fast and can be very overwhelming as there is much to unpack once you are out the other side. Imagine having ten thousand hours of therapy in twenty minutes. It is not a medicine that should be used recreationally or without the proper guidance.

Lastly, there is current concern in the community that there could be irreparable harm to the frog population due to the procurement of the medicine. Many believe we should turn to synthetic 5-MeO-DMT in order to ensure the frog population is not damaged in any manner.

There are legal clinics in Mexico that use synthetic 5meo-DMT and provide therapy, intention, and integration services. Access like this provides a great and safe opportunity for a wide array of people who can benefit from this medicine. My only concern with using synthetic is that while it can mimic the chemical structure, I question if it can really carry the same frequency as that what is naturally occurring in nature. This is a question I don't have the answer to, but I have my beliefs.

Psilocybin (Magic Mushrooms)

Psilocybin and psilocin are the active ingredient in "magic mushrooms." There are over 180 species of mushrooms that carry these psychoactive alkaloids. Mesoamerican cultures such as the Aztec, Mazatc, Mixtex, and Zapotecs have been using these fungi for thousands of years in sacred rituals.

These fungi gained notoriety in the western culture following a trip by American ethnomycologist R. Godon Wasson to Oaxaca, Mexico where he participated in a ceremony lead by Maria Sabina, a Mazatec curandera. Maria Sabina performed mushroom ceremonies for healing and divine connection. He later wrote about his experience in a national publication, and word spread across the Americas.

This sparked studies at major universities in the 1950's and 60's. For debatable reasons, the active ingredients were put on schedule 1 status, which halted all studies. Recently, there has been a resurgence in the study of the healing benefits of these fungi. Certain states have taken upon themselves to begin the legalization process, mainly in medical settings.

Dosage has a great deal to do with the experience when it comes to magic mushrooms. There are schools of thought with respect to microdosing, which is when one takes a dosage that does not induce the onset of a psychedelic experience but still might have therapeutic value, versus macrodosing, which is when one takes a dose which puts them into a psychedelic experience where many feel they reconnect with their spirit and nature. I am going to refrain from discussing dosage, as this is dependent on strains and concentration of active ingredients. Clinical research is showing promising results for the treatment of PTSD, depression, addiction, end of life anxiety, and trauma.

Iboga/Ibogaine

Iboga is derived from the root bark of the tabernanthe iboga shrub and considered a plant of sacred truth and vision. It is native to central West Africa and has been used for centuries as an ancestral medicine. The active compound in it is Ibogaine, which is a psychoactive indole alkaloid that induces what is said to be an extremely intense mental and physical experience lasting twelve to twenty-four hours, with lingering effects lasting a few days.

This medicine allows one to review their life in a manner not available by the other medicines. It is said to have profound effects on PTSD and addiction. There are several doctor-supervised facilities in Mexico that administer the medicine. Ibogaine acts on multiple neurotransmitters and has a unique ability to reset neural pathways associated with addiction.

Until recently, it has not been studied in the United States. However, that changed in 2025 when Texas passed a bill that will publicly and privately fund the study of Ibogaine to the tune of $100 million. This bill was spearheaded by former Governor Rick Perry after he heard the breakthroughs former armed services men and women had with their work with it and after his own personal journey with the medicine in Mexico.

MDMA

MDMA (3,4-Methylenedioxymethamphetaime) is a synthetic compound, but its roots trace back to safrole oil which is derived from the sassafras tree. It was first synthesized by Merck in 1912 but didn't enter popular culture until the 1970's when Dr. Alexander "Sasha" Shulgin resynthesized it, who was a psychopharmacologist. After using the medicine himself, he then shared it with psychotherapists who began using it as a therapeutic catalyst with patients.

At the same time, it also grew in popularity as a recreational party drug that enhanced dancing and connectivity. In 1984, the DEA moved to list MDMA as a schedule 1, which was accomplished in 1985. This was due to its widespread popularity and use in recreational settings.

MDMA has the effects of increased empathy, emotional openness, reduction of fear responses, enhanced trust, feelings of connection, and mild euphoria. The effects of a single dose can last for four to eight hours. While it is a human-designed synthetic, it can have profound heart-opening healing affects to assist in working through trauma, emotional blockages, relationships issues, and PTSD.

MAPS (Multidisciplinary Association for Psychedelic Studies) has led MDMA-assisted psychotherapy research since the 1980s, but unfortunately, it was dealt a major setback in achieving approvals from the FDA following their phase 3 trials in 2024. This would have led to a legal path for its use in psychedelic-assisted therapy in the U.S. John Hopkins, NYU, and other major universities have also used the substance in studies on its effects on trauma, depression, and end-of-life anxiety.

Lysergic acid diethylamide (LSD)

LSD is a semi-synthetic psychedelic that is derived from ergot which is a fungus that grows on rye and other grains. The active molecule is lysergic acid, which Albert Hoffman used to create LSD in a laboratory while working for Sandoz Laboratories in 1938. LSD has no indigenous roots.

In 1943, Albert Hoffman accidently absorbed a small amount into his skin and experienced unusual shifts in his perception. A few days later, he deliberately absorbed 250 micrograms, and this day later became known as Bicycle Day. On a bicycle ride home, he experienced the first intentional LSD trip.

LSD is considered a visionary amplifier and can assist with cosmic unity, creativity, and ego dissolution. It brings on powerful visual hallucinations, synesthesia (crossing of senses), altered sense of time, profound philosophical and mystical insights, and can aid in deep emotional release. These experiences can last upwards of twelve hours. It has been shown that LSD increases brain connectivity, dissolves rigid patterns of thought, and opens new doorways to expand one's consciousness.

In 1970, LSD was put on schedule 1, no medical benefits. Ironically, prior to this, there had been medical studies done at the government, university, and private business levels. It is now once again being studied by universities such as Johns Hopkins, NYU, and Imperial College London where they are exploring the use of LSD for end-of-life anxiety, depression, and creativity. Microdosing (tiny, sub-perceptual doses) has gained popularity in recent years, believed to enhance mood, focus, and creativity, though rigorous science is still emerging.

San Pedro (Huachuma) and Peyote (Mescaline)

San Pedro and Peyote are both species of cacti, and both have the same active compound, mescaline. Both have been used ritualistically for thousands of years. Peyote is sacred to Native American Tribes, and San Pedro has been used by Andean Shamans in the Andes.

From a ceremonial perspective, the buttons of the peyote plant are eaten or brewed into a bitter tea. The ceremonies are often guided and can be accompanied by a prayer around a fire. San Pedro is boiled into a green tea, and the ceremony often takes place in groups outdoors in nature. The experiences can last anywhere from eight to twelve hours.

Both cacti have similar healing benefits that can assist in treating depression, addiction, PTSD, and anxiety, but the studies are limited. Mescalin has been associated with increased openness, emotional catharsis, and enhanced wellbeing.

Mescaline is a schedule 1 compound. Peyote is legal in the U.S. to members of the Native American Church for religious use. San Pedro as a plant is legal, but once the mescaline is extracted, it is under schedule 1. Since peyote can take thirty years to grow to maturity, there are sustainability concerns and a belief that only members of the Native American Tribes should partake in its ceremonial uses.

My Journey with Entheogens

In my early life, I used many of these compounds recreationally without intent and not thinking about integration. However, this all changed when I entered the plant medicine community. I began to sit in ceremony and use certain medicines as supplements to help me heal emotionally and spiritually. I have already told a few stories about my interactions with Mother Ayahuasca, and I want to reiterate a point I have made several times. If you are not willing to do the work following the ceremony and sit in the fire of life, then the medicine will not help.

The medicine is catalyst on your journey. It can help with resolving personal and generational trauma, anxiety, depression, and other emotional, spiritual, mental, and even physical ailments. But it is up to the individual to do the work through integration and break the habits that don't serve them, separate from the people that aren't on their path to enlightenment, and have an honest conversation with oneself about what energies one allows in their life.

But let me make it personal. I have worked through many different challenges through my ceremony work. One that keeps coming up is my relationship with alcohol. I grew up in the business, and while I was never an alcoholic, I drank too much and too often.

While I was in undergraduate school, I promoted nightclubs in South Beach, Miami. When I returned to get my law degree and MBA, my network in the alcohol space and with club owners and promoters on South Beach was rather large. I began marketing alcohol brands at nightclubs and once again found myself ingrained in the culture. If you play your cards right the University of Miami offers two educations, one in the classroom and one in the streets. I benefited greatly from both.

I continued to work in the brand marketing space in South Florida following law school graduation and passing my bar. I started conceptualizing my own events focused on happenings like South Beach Food & Wine and Art Basel.

When I moved to Las Vegas, my position at Las Vegas Sands and Southern Glazers Wine and Spirits (formerly Southern Wine and Spirits) not only had me actively building the alcohol market but also had me indulging multiple nights a week. The behaviors one may acquire due to work may be detrimental to their overall well-being. It can be difficult to make that realization when all around you are exhibiting similar behaviors as it becomes a matter of degrees of depravity.

Something odd happened to me following the night of my first ayahuasca ceremony in Peru in 2016. My skin began to purge decades of alcohol intake. The smell coming from my pores was putrid, and it reminded me of the smell of the ground the morning after Fat Tuesday on Bourbon Street. This continued the entire week, to the point where I had to throw out all the clothes that I brought with me. No matter what I did, I couldn't get the smell out of them.

For about six months following these initial ceremonies, I was unable to physically lift an alcoholic beverage to my mouth. Eventually, I began to drink again, but not in the same manner. I had more awareness and began to understand that alcohol is a poison to the body, both physically and spiritually, but I still enjoyed drinking and wasn't ready to fully give it up. After all, the same can be said about sugar and caffeine.

About five years later I was in Puerta Morales, Mexico. I had come to do some medicine work with 5-Meo-DMT. While the shaman we sat with is not indigenous to this area, he had a global reputation in working with this medicine and is well respected in the community as curandera. He asked that I sit before my colleagues, as he didn't know me, and he had already worked with them in the past.

I inhaled the medicine and immediately crossed into the white light. The medicine was strong, and the experience was enlightening and magical. However, I noticed some odd things during the ceremony; first I felt the curandera pushing on my stomach with what felt like was a hot stone. While this gave me cause for concern, I allowed the ceremony to take its natural course and trusted him and the process. Second, there were a few Xoloitzcuintli dogs roaming the area, and during my ceremony they began to bark very loud, circle the mat I was on, and sniff around my face.

When I finally reoriented myself to my surroundings, I asked the curandera what had happened. Without hesitation he asked me, "You are around a lot of spirits, right?" And I said, "Yes, I have some psychic abilities." He laughed and said "No, I mean alcohol." He didn't know me, nor that I had spent a good portion of my adult life in the alcohol space as an executive and as a consumer.

He went on to tell me that that when we drink, we open ourselves up to spirits and their energy, something I already knew but never really wanted to hear. That is why we call them spirits. Many of these spirits look for vessels, humans, to keep them in the physical world. These energies can manifest in the host as pain, suffering, trauma, fear, and anxiety. I was one of those welcoming vessels.

He went on to explain that he was using the heated black obsidian on my stomach to cleanse the negative energy. The Xoloitzcuintli breed is the oldest in North America, and they are revered spirit guides that accompany souls on their journey to the afterlife. The medicine was pushing these energies out of me, and the dogs were helping them on their journey.

Why am I telling you this story? To highlight that we must do the work. I must be the one to head the messaging and understand that any alcohol use is detrimental to the purification of my mind, body and soul. In both instances, the medicine showed me that alcohol was detrimental to my physical, emotional, mental, and spiritual well-being. In all these years, I never fully committed to doing the work with respect to my relationship with alcohol, as I still enjoy a drink from time to time.

Following this ceremony, my relationship with alcohol changed once more. I have not completely cut it out of my life, but I rarely drink these days. I notice an immediate effect on my physical energy and my mental well-being during use and for days after. One can see how this also relates to discipline of our senses or lack thereof: essentially succumbing to the desires of the mundane world. I give myself grace to fall out of my discipline, but the medicine continually advises me against the use of alcoholic beverages. We must be honest with ourselves even when we prefer not to be, and choosing the path of pleasure and desire generally hinders our journey to enlightenment.

Regenerative Medicine: To Purify the Body

Overview

Prior to getting into the discussion of regenerative medicine, I want to make a few things clear. I have no medical training; however, through my own healing and business journey I was introduced to the world of regenerative medicine, specifically with respect to the use of Whartons Jelly to repair various injuries, diseases, and ailments. I am not offering any medical advice here, but rather giving an overview of the field from my personal experience as a patient, from my business experiences as an operator, and from my belief on how it aids in repairing damage to our body.

Regenerative medicine focuses on repairing, replacing, or regenerating human cells, tissues, or organs to restore normal or close to normal functionality. Rather than having surgery, it is generally done in a minimally invasive process through IV drips or direct injections.

Mesenchymal stem cells (MSC's) are at the forefront of the field of regenerative medicine. These cells are multipotent as they can differentiate into bone, cartilage, fat muscle, and nerve tissue. MSC's help the body to replace, repair, and regenerate cells that have become damaged over time and are currently being used to treat various medical conditions. Medical conditions such as orthopedic repair, neurological disorders, cardiovascular repair, autoimmune modulation, wound healing, and anti-aging.

So where does one find MSC's, or Wharton's Jelly? Wharton's Jelly is a gelatinous connective tissue found within the umbilical cord, surrounding the umbilical vein and arteries. It serves as a protective cushion for these blood vessels during pregnancy. Wharton's Jelly is a highly valuable source of mesenchymal stem cells (MSCs)—a type of multipotent adult stem cells.

While this is generally medical waste, the United States has draconian laws that prohibit them from being harvested and used in a widely accessible manner after a healthy birth. There is controversy about using Wharton's Jelly as it is harvested from umbilical cords after a healthy birth. MSC's harvested from the umbilical cord are called allogeneic MSC's. Currently in the United States, the FDA restricts use of the Whartons Jelly outside of approved clinical trials which are few and far between. Over the last 20+ years, we have seen other countries embrace this sector of medicine and exploding medical tourism businesses.

There are other regenerative healing treatments in the United States, and the most widely known would be using autologous stem cells. There are also various IV and injection cocktails that use exosomes, which are the signaling part of the stem cell but not the full cell. I am going to refrain from diving into the exosome discussion, as I do not have personal or professional experience other than conversations with doctors about their beliefs around efficacy. So, what is the difference, and why would one travel to a foreign jurisdiction for treatment?

Autologous stem cells are harvested from your own body prior to treatment. These cells are the same biological age as you. Over your lifespan, their replication rate diminishes, as does the strength of their healing capabilities. Think of how quick a child heals from a cut or another injury versus how long it may take someone in their forties; this is due to the efficacy of these cells as they age. Autologous stem cells have lower potency, are fewer in number, and have less regenerative capacity as compared to stems cells at time of birth. They also must be harvested from your bone marrow or fatty tissue, which can be painful and invasive. Lastly, your current health status also has a direct impact on their usefulness, once harvested, to assist in your current medical condition.

Allogeneic stem cells, Wharton's Jelly, are harvested from the tissue lining of the umbilical cord. This is done after a healthy childbirth. The donor cells are frozen. Prior to treatment, they then are replicated and prepared for the specific ailment the patient is being treated for and produced in large consistent batches under rigorous lab control. These cells are young, and have strong regenerative and immunomodulatory power. Immunomodulatory is the ability for these cells to modify or regulate the immune systems activity through stimulation if it is underactive or through calming it down if it is overactive. The function of these cells helps reduce inflammation and support tissue repair.

Many believe, and there are studies to support this belief, that Umbilical-cord-derived MSC's therapies are the most powerful and effective regenerative treatments available globally. They are also immune-privileged and do not trigger rejection, meaning they avoid or minimize attack from the immune system even when they are from another person. Lastly, dosing can be controlled and regulated and their viability rate, or survival rate after injection, is extremely high.

When choosing to explore regenerative medicine, several factors must be considered. You need to carefully research your options with respect to location, reputation of clinic/doctor, and financial investment that needs to be made. I can only speak from personal experience and say that these treatments have been a game changer. They have helped me repair injuries that I would have needed surgery for, aided in anti-aging efforts, and increased my overall physical fitness performance.

My Journey with Regenerative Medicine

"What do you know about stem-cells, and can you get on a plane to Colombia next week…?" An odd question from a business colleague, even odder being that most of the world was in some form of lockdown. But nonetheless, I booked a flight to Cali, Colombia. There, I met with some business colleagues, and we toured their legal cannabis fields before jumping in a car and driving to Periera, Colombia.

Periera is a beautiful city rich with culture, food, and national parks. I met with the local doctors, received my first stem-cell infusion, and learnt that Mesenchymal stem cell therapies are the cornerstone of regenerative medicine.

I saw an opportunity to be part of something financially lucrative and assist in healing people from all over the world.

MSC's focus is on healing the patient rather than creating a customer out of the patient. And so, Emuna Wellness was born. Emuna, as previously mentioned, means Faith in Hebrew, and at the time of this project I was reading the book *Garden of Emuna.*

We developed umbilical-cord-derived MSC protocols and procedures, working closely with local health authorities to ensure patient safety and treatment efficacy. We had a commitment to ethical and sustainable practices both in the production of MSCs from pre-screened donors to our unwavering commitment to the patient community we serve.

There were a great deal of hurdles to overcome. People were just starting to travel again, there was a high ticket to the procedure, and the consumer had to be properly educated. The team realized we had something special, and we all worked with ancestral medicine and now regenerative medicine. Through my own personal journey, I saw the benefits of working with ancestral medicine such as ayahuasca for the mind and spirit and using regenerative medicine for the trauma and injuries that were physical in nature in the body.

The front end of the business was to be purely regenerative medicine. But in looking at the global wellness tourism business, we wanted to incorporate ancestral medicine ceremonies as well. We were able to find a hacienda in town that would be perfect to host groups coming in for both modalities. While we were building out the regenerative medical offerings, we were also branding and planning for Emuna Ancestral, which would incorporate both modalities of healing.

I took the role as CEO & Co-Founder of the company and began reaching out to strategic partners in my network. My background in travel and hospitality allowed me to lay out a sales, marketing, and distribution plan. We would create a network of salespeople in verticals that complemented our offerings and had clients that can afford the procedures. Our network of sales representatives would be casino and nightlife hosts, luxury goods dealers from clothing to planes, celebrity athletes and influencers, real estate agents, and travel concierges to name a few. In return for their outreach to their existing clientele, we would close the deals and pay them a hefty commission.

The branding was done, the outreach list was done, and we started seeing out first clients. It was time to bring the salespeople down for what we called a "fam" trip. Basically, you give the house away to those individuals who are going to sell and carry the message to their networks. It also helps with content creation and testimonials which can be used in an omni-channel marketing strategy.

Covid dynamically changed the business world and how people operate as business goes, and the partners could not agree on the necessary capital raise. The principal partner didn't want to raise the necessary funds for the sales and marketing strategy to be put into play. He felt that the commission was enough incentive for these sales reps to promote into their network. I knew that was not practical or possible, and while the commission structure was more than sufficient, there were other aspects of that strategy that needed capital in order to trigger the sales team and sales. It was time to practice non-attachment. As mentioned, you either evolve or devolve; spiritually, physically, and ethically

Without proper funding, the business could not operate; however, I am still extremely grateful and appreciative for this experience and all the partners that were a part of its story. I gained the knowledge of regenerative medicine, developed and launched a global wellness tourism brand, and received several treatments to aid in the purification of my mind, body and soul. I also got to travel around Colombia and experience its rich culture.

In the coming years, I continued to explore the field. I went to Costa Rica and had treatments at a globally leading clinic to repair herniated discs in my back and neck. Injuries that I would have needed surgery are now a memory and the impediments they were causing to my physical fitness routine and mental well-being cease to exist.

Regenerative medicine, medicine 3.0, and functional medicine are finally getting the recognition on a global scale. In no way am I saying the current medical system in the United States should be discarded, but we need to look at the merging of the many fields and keep an open mind. It is my hope that umbilical cord MSC's are approved for greater use by the FDA in the United States, there is greater access, it is covered by insurance, and costs come down. It is a shame to think that something that is currently medical waste could be healing and helping millions upon millions of people.

Section 6 – Surrender

<u>Overview</u>

The very first thing I do when I wake up in the morning is light a candle. I light a candle to let the divine energy in, and I surrender myself to the day ahead. The concept of surrender does not mean to be a passive participant to life and let life happen to you. On the contrary, surrender is the concept of being an active participant, reducing resistance, and finding the flow of divine consciousness, thus allowing it to guide you.

Surrender allows one to transcend from lower frequencies of fear, anxiety, and grasping to higher frequences of truth, love, unity, empathy, and compassion, to get our personal frequencies in tune with the divine signal of consciousness. Too often, we let the little me, the small self, be the driver in our lives. The self, driven by ego, materialism, and worldly desires tries to guide our every move. When we surrender the small self, we open ourselves up to the divine self.

Surrender allows us to stop fighting life when it doesn't go our way. It allows us to flow with life using the tools of non-attachment and letting go, finding equanimity in all situations. When we fight life and attempt to manipulate the story line, we become rigid. We pull ourselves out of alignment and toward lower frequencies. It is through surrender that we use the momentum of divine consciousness to guide us through our day.

Our individual path becomes aligned with divine providence and our soul's purpose when we choose to surrender. We are able to raise our vibration and find inner peace when we relinquish the burden of control; dissolving fear and anxiety, we cultivate our trust in divinity. It is through this process that we begin to see obstacles as opportunities for growth, and rather than resist, we live in flow and cultivate resilience.

Surrender is the final step in stripping away our ego and living in flow with life. It invites us to stop fighting life and open our hearts so we may align with our higher calling and being. We must accept each moment as it presents itself in a non-judgmental manner, as it aligns us with the greatness of life that exists outside ourselves and outside of our ego. Once we surrender, life's opportunities flow like water, and the magic of life can blossom.

One of the hardest aspects of surrender is letting go of the ego. Our ego is what keeps us anchored in this world. While there is no reality to us living an egoless life, through surrender we can learn to let go of the aspects of our ego that keeps us anchored in negative situations and mindsets.

Our ego would like nothing more than to keep us separated from divine consciousness. Therefore, we must learn to refine the ego and place it in service of the soul rather than in service of our desires. The ego's job is to keep us attached to unnecessary desires which create cravings that do not serve our higher purpose. Through attachment to our desires, the ego uses our senses to keep us enslaved in the material world. When we recognize and remove these desires, we can loosen the ego's grip, and then the ego can perform the healthy function of assisting the soul in navigating the material world. It is the act of making the ego subservient rather than the dominant voice of our consciousness. Through surrender, the dominant voice becomes divine consciousnesses.

We need to remind ourselves to surrender when the ego speaks of life not being fair; materialism, desires, and other mindstuff only keep us from reaching higher frequencies. It is at these times we must take a moment to meditate, pray, and breathe. When we find our breath, we are able purify our mind and surrender to the moment. While the ego still exists, through surrender, we have silenced its noise, and through this silence we learn to live in the flow of life with divine consciousness.

When we learn to surrender control to life, we discard attachments to the imagined outcomes and attain greater wisdom through the intelligence of the universe. Too often, we fight the flow of life. We hold on to attachments and story lines that only bring us pain and suffering. Surrender allows us to go with the flow of life becoming one with the energy of divine consciousness. Through surrender, you become unattached to outcomes and make each momentary decision on the facts and energies as they present themselves. Surrender allows us to live in the present rather than regretting the past or fearing and forcing the future.

What surrender doesn't mean is to just let life knock you around or become passive to the happenings around you. Surrender is not an inactiveness; rather, it is an active state of living that is in cadence, rhythm, and frequency with your higher self and higher purpose. It is not giving up but rather letting go of all definitions we have of our ourselves and leaning into faith and trust.

Surrender is an active journey. One must let go of their desires. They must become non-attached to the story their ego tells them on how things should be or the expectations they might have. They must take time to align with higher frequencies through various modalities that return to breath.

When one surrenders, they come closer to self-realization, and they learn to understand that they are part of a greater energy. Surrender allows us to align with the synchronicities, creativity, and guidance of divine consciousness. It teaches us to slow down, reflect, be grateful, be appreciative, and realize how blessed we are in the present moment.

When we let go and let God, we surrender to the journey toward enlightenment. Through surrender we arrive at the self-realization that you are born into the situation of trials and tribulations that are ordained by divine consciousness for your greatest souls' correction. And we can fully realize who we are meant to be.

The Victim and Surrender

It is difficult for the victim to surrender, as they view it as a loss of control or weakness. They do not feel supported by anyone or anything. In their mind, everyone and everything works against them or is out get them. Ego dominates the victim through survival-based desires, stripping them of their will and power.

The victim's prayer and meditation practices are colored by fear, anger, worry, and hopelessness. They do not understand that these tools aid in their surrender to divinity. Rather they pray from a place of desperation, as a last resort. They fail to have gratitude for all the blessings that have already been bestowed upon them.

In their meditation, they cannot silence the sense telephones, their mind is constantly racing. Rather than turn within they sit in their pain and suffering, they revel in their trauma rather than surrender, and they live in fear and resistance.

If the victim would surrender to the flow of life, they feel they would be opening themselves up to pain, abandonment, and disappointment. They lack faith and trust in divine consciousnesses and would rather remain attached to the pain and suffering they have found comfort in then surrender. There is just no room for them to be vulnerable.

The Survivor and Surrender

Unlike the victim, the survivor recognizes that control is limited but is unable to fully practice non-attachment and letting go and therefore cannot fully surrender. They still carry the scars of their past trauma and do not want to fully commit to being hurt again. They feel if they surrender completely, they will be unable to protect themselves from negative experiences.

While the survivor has faith in a higher power, they are unwilling to fully surrender to divinity's guidance as they are still grappling with the concept of trust. Why should they trust that all things happen for a reason when they have had to endure so much pain and suffering in the past? After all, they are the ones, in their mind, who pulled themselves through the fire. They fail to recognize that divine consciousness is beside them and within them. They have not fully come to terms with the concept that bad things happen to good people for their greatest good. Survivors feel they are the only ones they can really trust as they are the ones they believe carry themselves over the hurdles and through the obstacles of life.

The survivor's prayers are still tied to desired outcomes. This is part and parcel because they are still struggling with trust. They expect their prayers to be answered in the way they asked, and when they are not, they feel betrayed and let down. But as they saying goes, God works in mysterious ways. Many times, the survivor fails to recognize that their prayers are being answered because they are not being answered in the manner they requested, so they feel let down. We don't always know what it is we need to carry on and elevate our consciousness, but we are always protected and provided for when we surrender.

It is also difficult for the survivor to fully surrender during meditation. If they fully surrender during meditation, they are no longer in control. They feel this can open themselves up to inability to defend themselves from negative things happening to them. They never can fully relax and detach themselves from their sense telephones as they feel they always need to be on guard to prevent any further traumatic events from occurring.

Rather, they choose to surrender only when they can align their egos' desires, and they feel they can protect themselves. This can be an exhausting process and they waver between tension and release. Often, surrender only comes due to the exhaustion of trying to manipulate the outcome. Surrender is meant to be a spiritual practice, and surrender due to exhaustion is only a strategy for relief.

The survivor fails to recognize that through surrender they become divinely protected. They no longer need to worry about negative things occurring to them as they will be in flow with the energy of the universe. The determination of negative or positive is something the ego assigns to events that happened to us and around us. Through surrender, we relinquish the ego and realize that there is no negative and positive; only lessons to guide us on our journey to enlightenment. The survivor never fully surrenders and therefore never fully enters the flow state of life or reaches equanimity as they still fear losing control.

The Warrior and Surrender

Through discipline, non-attachment, faith, trust, and letting go of what no longer serves them, the warrior surrenders to the flow. They have put their ego in check and in service as an aid to only desire what is needed on their journey to enlightenment. Surrender allows the warrior to be in alignment with higher frequencies, and through each lesson and each fire they raise their vibration and purify their mind, body, and soul.

Each day begins with prayer and gratitude. Their prayer is filled with gratitude for all the blessings divine consciousness has and continues to bestow upon them, and their meditation disconnects their sense-telephone so they may begin the day with the ritual purification of their mind. Through this practice they surrender to the energy of the day with blessings, gratitude, and appreciation.

It is through non-attachment that the warrior has come to disassociate from people, places, and things that no longer serve them. The warrior has chosen to let go of the stories that cause negative feelings, emotions, pain, and suffering. Through their process of non-attachment and letting go, they have found surrender and now live life in equanimity. It was through the process of the surrender that the warrior sits in the fire of life and becomes one with the fire.

The warrior has learned that surrender does not mean to give up, but rather it means to live a disciplined life through their spiritual practice, nutritional behavior, physical fitness routine, and relationship with self and others. What does this mean? It means they have put aside their desires and have chosen to focus on activities, beliefs, and energies that aid them in the purification of their mind, body, and soul and on their journey to enlightenment.

They understand that they are a spirit having a human experience, and that through surrender, they connect their physical body to the spiritual world and divine consciousness. While they are aware of the separation between the mundane and spiritual worlds, they know the final act of surrender will harmonize the two. And with their faith and trust in divinity, they are willing let go and let God, understanding this is the path to their soul's correction.

Surrender is allowing divine consciousness to guide you on the journey to enlightenment that you are meant to be on rather than the one you thought you should be on. It is to live in harmony with life, nature, and truth, and to stop forcing outcomes. One is aided on their journey through the practice of discipline, faith, and trust and the use of the tools of non-attachment, letting go, meditation, and prayer. Surrender is the understanding that higher states of consciousness emerge not from forcing, but from releasing. Surrender to who you are supposed to be, not who you want to be or who thought you should be.

My Journey to Surrender

Surrender is something I continue to work on throughout my life. My personal life and business life have always been intertwined. It was through several experiences in my career that I finally surrendered to my calling, and I am sitting here writing this book. I had prayed for many of these experiences to manifest; however, how they manifested was not what I had anticipated.

And it was through these experiences or obstacles that I gained faith and trust in divine consciousness. I found my discipline and learned to practice non-attachment and letting go. Without these experiences, I would not be the man I am today. With each experience I grew wiser and let go of expectations. Through surrender, I realized how blessed, grateful, and appreciative I was, am, and will continue to be. It was through these experiences that I truly learned the meaning of the word surrender.

Three major global events had a dramatic impact on the course of both my personal and professional career. Living through these experiences in some cases caused me a great deal of pain, fear, anxiety, and trauma. However, once I shifted my perspective, I began to see them as my greatest teachers.

I want to return to the discussion of my experience on 9/11/01. The events of this day cannot be minimized. This was a global traumatic event, one that I experienced personally. Families lost loved ones, businesses were destroyed, and our idea of safety and security as Americans was swiftly shattered. My experience of not only being there but it also being my first day of work out of college was something that seemed out of a movie.

To say this took a long time to process would be an understatement. Through the years, I went through a laundry list of emotions as well as coping mechanisms, coping mechanism that toxified my mind, body, and soul even further.

The aspect of surrender came years after the experience itself. I had never surrendered my expectations of how I thought that day should have gone and what might have transpired if this horrific terrorist attack hadn't happened. Would I have stayed in NYC? Would I have had a successful financial career? How would have my story differed if that day occurred as I prayed for? What if I had not seen that much death and destruction firsthand? Well, the hard truth is that it doesn't really matter.

My soul's correction put me there on that day. I was supposed to go through the experience and work through all the trauma it caused. It was supposed to shake me, it was supposed to break me, and it was supposed to make me pivot time and time again for the next two decades. And lastly, it was supposed to make me emotionally stronger than I ever could have imagined, and it did.

Once I properly processed the happenings of this day, I began to look back on it with gratitude. I surrendered and accepted that it was meant to be a part of my story. I am grateful for how 9/11 shaped my future, the course correction it sent me on, and the future opportunities it bestowed upon me to help myself and others transcend such unthinkable experiences.

Many things can be said about traumatic experiences, but one must trust that whatever divine consciousness brings into our life is for our soul's correction and was meant to occur. Even under the most horrific circumstances, we must align with the light and reach for higher frequencies.

Now it was the summer of 2008, and I accepted an offer to work for Las Vegas Sands. *Casino* is one of my favorite movies, and I started to think about the life that was ahead of me, full of glitz, glam, money, and deal-making. And to think when I first came to Las Vegas in 2002, I said I would never come back.

I arrived ready to learn the business and its intricacies. The goal was to implement my business and legal expertise and create 360-degree partnership deals. This would create new profit centers for an already thriving business enterprise and access to a greater net of customers. Unfortunately, the week I started, the mortgage crisis hit a new low, the stock market crashed, and we entered one of the biggest recessions in history. Ironically, Lehman Brothers filed for bankruptcy—yes, Lehman Brothers, the company I worked for on 9/11/01. LVS stock went down to $2, and people were more concerned about saving their departments and jobs than working with a new executive on an unproven model.

At the time, the experience was brutal. I technically didn't report to any department. I wasn't properly onboarded in a manner that would have made the necessary departments friendly to my arrival. This was a key factor to the success of partnerships as multiple departments needed to buy-in to the strategy for it to work. Given what was going on in the markets and company, there was little to no interest in anyone putting their neck on the line if they weren't told to and had to. But I was a fighter, and so I made my own way.

When I look back, there were many times I could have quit and given up. But I choose to surrender to the situation that I landed in and learn from it. Through my tenure at LVS, I forged new business models, created new business units, and grew my leadership and communication skills. Had I not surrendered to the experience I was put in, I would have missed out on this pivotal point in my career. Once again, I learned that we need to let go of our expectations and surrender to the flow of the experience divinity places us in.

In 2016, I decided to explore getting into the cannabis space, and in 2018 I dove off the cliff without a net. CannaFAME was born based on my thought process of developing brands in a similar fashion to how those are developed in the alcohol industry. Rather than owning a facility or acquiring a license, we would develop the brands and outsource the procurement, assembly, and distribution. From a financial perspective, this would alleviate the heavy cost of the operations, and from a legal perspective, this would make us an IP company rather than a cannabis company. Everyone in the space was trying different business models due to the dissonance in the laws; however, given my experiences in the alcohol space, I saw striking similarities to the path of development of brands.

CannaFAME was a brand development and incubation company that incubated, owned, and operated innovative global cannabis brands across lifestyle platforms, including fashion, art, music, and entertainment. CannaFAME specialized in taking brands from concept to market. My older siblings liked the concept, and given where they were at in their careers, thought it would be a good family gamble to go all in as a team. We decided to pool our funds and forgo salaries to get the brands to market. This would allow us to gain a better valuation prior to bringing on outside capital.

Higher Frequencies (HF) was the first brand conceptualized in the portfolio, and over the years it has morphed into many things, as brands do. It was to be a cannabis brand, a vehicle for change, a vehicle for healing, a platform, a clothing line, a distribution portal for all things whole-life wellness, festivals, resorts, retreats, residences, blah blah blah. Maybe it will be all these things, maybe it will be some of these things, maybe maybe maybe.

A family member, captain of industry and mentor, may he rest in peace, who I hold in high regard, used to always say "MAYBE" when I would run something by him. I finally realized he was telling me to surrender. And as I sit here and pen this manifesto, I have had to fully surrender to what I thought Higher Frequencies was meant to be.

In its inception, it was the lead cannabis brand in the portfolio created by myself and my family. Based on the solfeggio frequencies and chakras, we took the botanicals associated with each and combined them with various cannabinoids creating seven distinct blends that could be pressed into various form factors such as vapes, edibles, and tablets. There was also a clothing component. The design team I worked with for HF and its sister brands had previously worked with brands such as Yeezus, Fear of God, Vitamin Water, Adidas, Nike, and Undefeated. They somehow were able to get what was in my head on to the computer screen, and eventually the products and shelves.

I moved to California to develop the brands, the supply chain, and the necessary relationships in the market. My family handled the legal, financial, and operations out of South Florida. We conceptualized two other brands.

Hesh's was named after our grandfather who was a war hero and the local fruit man in Brighton Beach, Brooklyn New York. For Hesh's, we worked with Humboldt farmers to deliver outdoor cannabis flower in various sku's under a collective model such as found in the agriculture or the wine business, highlighting the farms and the farmer's stories under the Hesh's name. The plan was also to launch flavored supplements that drew inspiration from local flavor profiles specific to the region the brand would be found in.

And lastly, Generic Cannabis, which would take branding cues from the streetwear community and follow a similar pattern as Kirkland, Costco's in-house value driven brand, essentially delivering high quality cannabis products under a "Generic" label at a lower cost to the consumers. Higher Frequencies would be our affordable/approachable luxury brand, Hesh's would be our mid-tier/standard brand, and Generic would be our value-drive brand. We would go to market able to satiate the three core price categories.

For two years, we grinded it out and we were ready to go to market. All legal documents were signed with the contract manufacturers, all product and parts were in transit or already in process of assemblage, and we had aligned with a great distributor. There were many bumps along the way, but we made it, or so we thought. I had a great road map from the alcohol industry on the vision of the company and how we needed to move to become a brand house like Sidney Frank, Diageo, Pernod Ricard, and Beam Global.

Just as we were about to launch, the distributor of record went out of business. I quickly pivoted us into another distributor. We were ready to go with 50,000 units and eight skus across the three brands. We soft launched into a number retail accounts, and everyone loved the brands, especially Higher Frequencies. We were one month out from Hall of Flowers, where we would show off the brands to the entire California cannabis industry, the center of the cannabis world. And then Covid came crashing down on us all. First it was just noise. And one month before Hall of Flowers, the world went into lockdown, especially California.

We were unable to get the brands in front of the necessary buyers. There was no opportunity for consumer discovery for the next twelve months as events, gatherings, and happenings were essentially outlawed. While we had some capital runway, we needed sales so we could rebuild inventory, or we needed an investment. We were getting good traction with Generic, but due to a defect in the manufacturing of the pens, they began to leak, and we lost consumer confidence. The only option was to exit the market and protect the intellectual property for a later time.

With respect to business, almost everything came to a griding halt. The cannabis business continued to be plagued with banking, funding, and consumer touch point issues. However, there was a loophole in the hemp laws which allowed the sale of certain psychoactive ingredients derived from the Hemp plant to be manufactured, distributed, and sold through non-regulated smoke shops.

Over the next few years, I worked on some Hemp brands as the law was a bit laxer. I created a brand house focused on brands in this space exclusively. However, the players in this space were not good actors, there was lots of counterfeiting, and many distributors took it upon themselves not to pay their bills. All through this time, I was going deeper and deeper into my wellness journey and constantly thinking about Higher Frequencies.

Many friends and family recognized all the work that I had done and often came to me for advice. Several of them recommended I start coaching people. At first, I didn't like the idea of this as I felt it was my mission to share the knowledge that I had garnered with those whose path I crossed without the want of reciprocity. But a friend had been assisting others in developing coaching programs, so I thought I'd give it a shot. I started to create content. However, for a myriad of reasons, I didn't feel aligned with the selling myself online. The market was flooded with charlatans.

During the same time, I was traveling back and forth from La to Las Vegas, my former home. The idea of moving back to Las Vegas presented itself in my many conversations with friends and colleagues. And in February of 2024, I decided to make the move, not sure what I was going to do but confident it was time move on. I just knew I had to surrender.

Oddly enough, Las Vegas was having its own wellness awakening. People were diving deep into health and spiritualty. I always felt there was an energy here that needed to be cultivated, but it seemed extremely different this time around. The city itself was also going through another metamorphosis. With the addition of major sports teams, F1, and the development of the suburbs, Las Vegas was becoming more than a tourist destination. Las Vegas was a thriving economy and U.S. city that people from all sorts of places and backgrounds now called home.

I soon found myself in a few development discussions about wellness communities, resorts, residences, and smart cities. The overall theme in these conversations was the yearning for those to have wellness options in the tourism and residence sector. Places where people could, gather, learn, and integrate. Places that could help them heal physically, spiritually, and emotionally. And many felt, including myself, that Las Vegas was the perfect city with its mix of business and leisure visitors, being the sports and entertainment capital of the globe, having proximity to so many outdoor destination sites and cities, and the ease of use of its international airport.

You see, we talk about integration, but we move further away from surrounding ourselves with the necessary community that can assist in the process. Take my case for example. I have traveled the globe to sit with ancestral medicine and have regenerative medicine treatments. With my own will and the support of my mentors, some of which I have never met, I integrate daily the lessons that have and continue to be bestowed upon me into my life. But many are not as fortunate, many do not have the self-discipline, and many do not have the will. I am not passing judgement, but making an observation.

While I was exploring this, I decided to record a few Higher Frequencies podcast episodes and rebrand the social media and website. This allowed me to further surrender to what I thought Higher Frequencies was and how I was going to spark the fire for HF to become what I knew it was supposed to be.

I continue to push forward on discussions and opportunities surrounding residential and resort projects in Las Vegas that I hope will shape the future of the city and be examples for other cities to follow. Smart Cities that focus on sustainability, regenerative living and whole-life wellness. There is a long road ahead of us to get this accomplished, but I am hopeful that divinity will guide me. I accept it as my mission, and I follow the path G-D has laid out in front me. I don't always see where the road leads, but the road less traveled is the one for me.

And in my meditations, I felt it was time for me to pen my learnings to share with others. We are all born into our situation for our greatest souls' correction; no matter your religion, your economic situation, or any other thing that can be used as an excuse or label of some sort, you must have faith in a higher power and trust that all things that show up in your life are part of your soul correction. Through surrender I found my calling, to share my knowledge, Higher Frequencies.

Part 5

In Closing

Memento Mori x Pura Vida

"You Can Leave Life Right Now...So Live your Best Life." IO

Too often, we get caught in the drama of our own life. The trauma one experiences turns to baggage that we must unload and move past. As we work through our discipline and use the tools presented in the previous chapters, it is helpful to remember that life is finite, and you must live in the present moment. While striving for a better you, you must also be grateful for your current situation and proud of who you are at any given moment.

Up to this point, we have discussed the how. How can discipline help us on our journey toward enlightenment? How can we control our senses to turn within and discover divine consciousness? How can we live a more disciplined life? How can we purify our mind body and soul? How can various tools such as non-attachment, letting go, faith and trust, and meditation and prayer aid us in achieving our goals? But we have yet to discuss the why.

Why should we strive for a more disciplined life? Why is it important to find meaning in the struggle? Why should one want to burn off what no longer serves them? Why must we purify our mind body and soul to reach higher frequencies? Why should we limit the control our desires have over us in the mundane world? Why, why, why?

I'd like to introduce two sayings that come from cultures and centuries apart, but when read collectively, embody my thought process on how precious our human life is and how important it is we live it to the fullest with love, light, and sincerity in our actions with respect to ourselves and others. Words that give us the strength to move, the determination to stay strong, and the awareness of how blessed we are to be a spiritual being having a human experience. Sayings, when combined, keep us centered on gratitude and appreciation for our breath and its connectivity to divinity. Memento Mori, a stoic philosophy, from the age of antiquity and Pura Vida from the people, culture, and energy of Costa Rica. The WHY.

Memento Mori is as a phrase from the time of antiquity and one that the Stoics such as Seneca highlighted in various writings and philosophies. It is an anchor of stoicism and the teachings of that time and is timeless in its meaning. Memento Mori loosely translates to "remember you must die." in other words, you could leave life right now. It is reminder of the fragility of the human experience and that any moment in time death could be lurking around the corner.

One might say this is a somber thought, but it is not; it is reality. And more important it is a reminder that you should never take your health and your ability to love, to live, and to experience this life for granted. You are blessed to be here, so live each moment with gratitude. We are given this body to live our lives to the fullest and not to lament on the hardships of what obstacles life may present, but rather to embrace obstacles as growth experiences. Ultimately, be grateful for the life we have and the path we are on because death can be around the corner at any moment.

Memento Mori reminds us that this life and all things that happen around us and to us are blessings. Even things we perceive as curses are blessings. It is our curses, our hardships, that are our greatest teachers. When hard times fell on these great stoic philosophers, they leaned into them, they didn't complain. It fueled their beliefs in divinity and through the curse they uncovered lessons, the gems, or some might say blessings that allowed them to become better versions of themselves. No matter what was happening around them or to them, they leaned into their discipline and found the divine light of consciousness through the darkness, because tomorrow isn't promised and divinity doesn't give its warriors anything they cannot handle. Memento Mori reminds us that our time here is finite, which fuels the discipline to focus on what truly matters: our soul's correction and our journey toward enlightenment.

Pura Vida is a saying that embodies the people and culture of Costa Rica and loosely translates to pure life or the simple life. But it is much more than that, as anyone who has visited Costa Rica can attest. These two words are a way of living and symbolize life, a mantra, and a state of being. It is the embodiment that no matter what is going on in life, you need to take a moment smile at yourself, smile at others, and come from a center of love, gratitude, and appreciation. The fact that you get to walk on this earth and experience all the emotions that come with being a human is a blessing. We must remove ourselves from the noise and negativity of the days current events and news to remind ourselves how blessed we really are. PURA VIDA!

If we are aware life is not promised and we must make the best of every moment, then why would one be concerned about the material aspects of life? Why would one be a slave to our sense telephones searching for momentary gratification rather than eternal bliss? When we realize all this is temporary, we have an awareness that all our behaviors, actions, and habits either help us reach higher frequencies and aid us in our journey to enlightenment. Or our behaviors, actions, and habits deter us, detract us, and impede us from reaching higher frequencies on our journey to enlightenment.

We create an awareness that life is precious through the practice of discipline. Tomorrow is not promised, and we must work daily to purify our mind, body, and soul. Each act of discipline reminds us of this. Whether it be in your spiritual practice, nutritional behavior, physical fitness routine, or relationship with self and others, we recognize the gift the present is, and we choose to live our best life in healing and helping ourselves and others.

This is the intersection of Memento Mori and Pura Vida: to heal and repair the world and all that is in and a part of it, creating strength and healing in the collective consciousness of the universe. It is no wonder we have a mental health crisis as we have strayed from this concept. People are chasing externalities, searching for happiness in material items, and stepping on and around each other to satiate momentary desires.

Real happiness is within and in the company of those you love and those that love you. It is seeing all humankind work as one to deliver light in and between us all. You cannot take things with you when you die, you cannot take your stature, you cannot take your possessions, you cannot take your position, you cannot take your point of view; all you can take is your soul, and it is up to you to feed it with light and love. This is why we practice discipline.

As we lean into our discipline, we become more appreciative for all the light that shines on us emotionally, physically, and spiritually. This, to me, is where these two 'life slogans' intersect. It is in the cold and constant reminder of "Memento Mori" and the warmth and light of "Pura Vida" that we are reminded that at any moment of life, our fire, can be extinguished so we must live our best life and make every moment count.

The journey to enlightenment is a privilege, not a right. You have breath and body, and through it you have the opportunity to align your soul to divine consciousness. We do not know when we will leave this existence, so why waste one moment on low frequency energies such as fear, anxiety, and depression?

Every moment is a moment to learn, to say I love you, to say thank you, and to practice gratitude. These moments must be embraced as if they were your last, so live your best life, treat yourself and others with kindness, love, and respect. The fact that you are alive, breathing, and healthy is the ultimate blessing. Use your breath, energy, and frequencies wisely as they are precious, they are gift; as they say, "That is why it is called the 'present.'"

The Frequency of Love

Love is the understanding that you are divine consciousness; you can turn within to connect to this unlimited source energy and share this energy with others without the want of reciprocity.

Vibrating on the Frequency of Love.

I love myself, I love others, I love all. I love.

My love unifies and empowers.

The concept of love is often spoken of in popular culture, science, and religion. There are courses taught about love, songs written about love, movies made about love, and books penned about love. However, most of the modern discussion of love deals with externalities such as people, places, things we possess, and the conditions we place upon them. Love, to most, is a belief on how they should receive love and how they should give love, which is conditional. Most see love as a call and response between individuals rather than a frequency between our spirit and the universe.

The frequency I am speaking of is 639HZ. It is the frequency of love, connection, and harmonious relationships. It is the fabric of how we interact with ourselves and the world. It should be of no surprise that much of the world is in pain and suffering, when most cannot articulate what the frequency of love is how it is to be attracted. Love is attracted through the self-realization that you are love, you are the divine source, and this frequency of love is an unlimited energy that is within you when you connect to divine consciousness.

You can stop searching for love in others. You can stop searching for love through your five senses. Rather, when you practice discipline, turn within, cultivate the frequency of love, and share it without the want of reciprocity, you realize you are love, and you attract all the love you will ever need.

The frequency of love is unconditional and unlimited; it is not the conditional love one feels from the dopamine boost they experience through their senses and externalities. The frequency of love promotes love, unity, and harmony. It encourages forgiveness, compassion and empathy. This frequency can heal broken relationships, attract harmonious connections, and deepen understanding between people. The frequency of love does all this without conditions, unconditionally.

Love is the present moment; it is the unconditional exchange of divine consciousness between souls having a human experience to aid them on their journey to enlightenment. Love is the healing of wounds that go unspoken. Love is family. Love is friends. Love is the moments you share with other that connects you to divine consciousness. To love is to heal, to learn, to enlighten, and to grow spiritually, emotionally, and mentally.

You must love yourself first. Love yourself so much that you no longer accept people, places, habits, or behaviors that lower your frequency. By loving yourself, you connect to divine consciousness and open yourself up to the unlimited healing and love of the universe. Once you love yourself, you can help others learn to love and heal themselves, and through the process the global community can began to heal. When we love, we put aside judgement, as we see all beings as an extension of the universe. We come to the realization that when I judge another, I am merely judging myself. We can choose to love with open hearts and minds rather than judge, moving from the lower frequency of judgment to the higher frequencies of love, empathy, and compassion.

"I want to cultivate the energy of love within me and share it unconditionally." Love is one of the greatest stimulants in the world. Whatever I do, I do with the greatest love I have in me, the frequency of love. When we choose to love we do not become fatigued, we don't live in fear, we cease to cultivate the energies of shame and anxiety. Under the influence of love the will can do almost anything. This is the frequency we should strive to connect to, cultivate, share, and attract.

When we discipline our senses to purify our minds, bodies, and souls through our spiritual practice, nutritional behavior, physical fitness routine, and relationship with self and others, ultimately, we cultivate the frequency of love. It is through our discipline that we can silence our sense telephones and reconnect to divine consciousness. And through this we ultimately surrender to the frequency of love. Love becomes the frequency that guides on our journey to enlightenment. When we vibrate on the frequency of love, we live in equanimity.

I decided years ago I never again want to fall in love. We RISE IN LOVE when we cultivate the frequency of love from within and share it unconditionally. I don't want to fall in love with my soulmate, I don't want to fall in love with material items such as cars or jewelry, I don't want to fall in love with love, and I don't want to fall in love with my life. Why would I ever want to fall, lower, diminish something that is meant to enlighten, elevate, and heal?

I want to RISE IN LOVE. When I rise in love with myself, I learn from my past, I live in the present, and I see a future of light and love. A present and future devoid of limiting beliefs, pain, and suffering. I rise in love with my partner; we create new energy to heal ourselves and others. We embark on the adventure of life together with unlimited light and love. When you love someone deeply, you will see all people as part of that love. When I rise in love with my friends, family, and colleagues, we burn away the energies of fear, anxiety, hate, and jealousy. When we rise in love, we reach higher frequencies, and love becomes the fuel for our journey to enlightenment. May we all vibrate on the frequency of love individually and collectively

Now do you understand why you must practice discipline.... To Rise in Love, To Vibrate on the Frequency of Love...to always be in motion toward Higher Frequencies....

A Prayer for Your Journey To Enlightenment
Calling in the Guidance of Our Ancestors

Through my discipline and my daily practice, I call in
the healing, support, guidance, light, and love of divine
consciousness and the spirits of my ancestors.

To the East, we call Archangel Michael and the element of fire.
Angel of Mercy, The Prince of Light,
Representing and bringing forth the energies of love, strength,
and protection.
Protect and lead us in spiritual warfare, bring us divine light
and guidance so we may practice discipline in the mundane
world.
With Abraham and Sarah, who walked into new beginnings,
may strength and kindness rise with the dawn.

To the south, we call Raphael and the element of water.
Angel of Healing and Renewal
Messenger of God, Guardian of the inner world and intuition.
Symbolizing clarity, revelation, and guidance from the divine.
Deliver to us important messages and revelations to purify our
mind, body, and soul.
With Isaac and Rebecca, may the fire of resilience and devotion
warm and restore my spirit....

To the west, we call Gabrial and the element of air.
Angel of Courage and Truth
Symbolizing divine health, peace, and protection on our
journey to enlightenment
Heal us and remind us that there is no separation between our
soul and divine consciousness, we are one in the same.
With Jacob, Rachel, and Leah, may dreams, justice, and family
guide us as the sun sets.

To the North, we call Uriel and the element of earth.
Angel of Light and Wisdom & Knowledge
Symbolizing divine truth, clarity, and wisdom in times of
darkness
Set fire to what no longer serves us and illuminate the path of
righteousness
With our Ancestors who endured exile and carried the hidden
spark of divinity, may we find guidance in the unseen and
courage in the dark.

Above me and below me, before me and behind me, within me
and around me,
May the love of my ancestors and the guardianship of the angels
encircle me in peace, compassion and empathy.
Divine Consciousness—hold me in your embrace.
May we continue to rise in love and attain higher frequencies.